THE *Refiner's Fire*

To order additional copies of *The Refiner's Fire,*
by Gavin Anthony, **call 1-800-765-6955.**

Visit us at www.reviewandherald.com
for information on other Review and Herald® products.

THE *Refiner's Fire*

GAVIN ANTHONY

▶ IN ALL THINGS *God* WORKS FOR GOOD ◀

REVIEW AND HERALD® PUBLISHING ASSOCIATION
Since 1861 | www.reviewandherald.com

Unless otherwise noted, all Scripture references are from the *Holy Bible, New International Version.* Copyright © 1973, 1978, 1984, International Bible Society. Used by permission of Zondervan Bible Publishers.

Scripture quotations marked NASB are from the *New American Standard Bible,* copyright © 1960, 1962, 1963, 1968, 1971, 1972, 1973, 1975, 1977, 1994 by The Lockman Foundation. Used by permission.
Scripture quotations marked NKJV are from the New King James Version. Copyright © 1979, 1980, 1982 by Thomas Nelson, Inc. Used by permission. All rights reserved.
Scripture quotations marked NLT are taken from the *Holy Bible,* New Living Translation, copyright © 1996. Used by permission of Tyndale House Publishers, Inc., Wheaton, Illinois 60189. All rights reserved.
Bible texts credited to NRSV are from the New Revised Standard Version of the Bible, copyright © 1989 by the Division of Christian Education of the National Council of the Churches of Christ in the U.S.A. Used by permission.

This book was
Edited by Gerald Wheeler
Copyedited by James Cavil
Cover designed by Ron Pride
Cover art by Lars Justinen, www.goodsalt.com
Typeset: 11/13 Bembo

PRINTED IN U.S.A.
11 10 09 08 07   5 4 3 2 1

Library of Congress Cataloging-in-Publication Data
Anthony, Gavin, 1967-   .
    The refiner's fire : in all things, God works for good / Gavin Anthony.
      p. cm.
    ISBN 978-0-8280-2007-7
1. Suffering—Religious aspects—Christianity. 2. Christian life. I. Title.
    BV4909.A58 2007
    248.8'6—dc22

                                                    2007005565

DEDICATION

To Jenny and Robyn

Who can understand how our simple acts of kindness
will impact the rest of eternity?

*"The Lord Jesus is making experiments on human hearts
through the exhibition of His mercy and abundant grace. He
is effecting transformations so amazing that Satan, with all
his triumphant boasting, with all his confederacy of evil
united against God and the laws of His government, stands
viewing them as a fortress impregnable to his sophistries and
delusions. They are to him an incomprehensible mystery. The
angels of God, seraphim and cherubim, the powers commis-
sioned to cooperate with human agencies, look on with astonishment and joy, that fallen men, once children of wrath, are
through the training of Christ developing characters after the
divine similitude, to be sons and daughters of God, to act an
important part in the occupations and pleasures of heaven."*

—*Ellen G. White*, Testimonies to Ministers, *p. 18.*

CONTENTS

INTRODUCTION

To be honest, this book is an accident. I never set out to study the role of suffering in our lives, but as I began to enter into some of life's crucibles myself, I started to take notes.

The book itself began as a series of apparently unconnected prayers. I had been going through a long stressful period in which I changed jobs and moved to a new country. It resulted in my prayer life becoming quite barren, for I had been unconsciously trading busyness for communion with God. Eventually a longing began to well up from within to recover some of my lost passion for prayer.

To help rekindle this desire, I bought a book on prayer by Evelyn Christensen, whose best-selling book, *What Happens When Women Pray,* had taught me to pray as a 15-year-old. As I read a chapter on God's glory being supreme, I began to feel a hunger for this once again to be my own experience. Later I wrote in my spiritual journal how I really wanted to serve God with everything I was and how I realized as never before that at the heart of glorifying God is sacrifice. "Total devotion," I promised God rather naively, "no matter the cost."

Four days later I received an e-mail to present a seminar at the 2001 European Ministers' Council entitled "Prayer in the Life of the Pastor: How to Survive Spiritually." I then prayed my second wildly naive prayer, asking God to teach me during the next 10 months what He wanted me to pass on to the pastors. "Be glorified in my life, whatever the cost," I concluded.

I prayed with sincerity, but felt a pang of caution. If I was to teach others about "surviving," would I perhaps myself experience the strains of what it meant just to survive?

I was right. Within days everything seemed to start falling apart. When it came down to it, this certainly wasn't my idea of how to glorify God. However, as the months rolled by, what God began to teach me was exactly the material I needed for the seminar. And from that resulted the birth of this book.

Yet I think that in God's mind the book began many years before. While working through an earlier draft, I suddenly remembered a prayer from more than 10 years before. Working in Albania just after the fall of Communism, I had listened hour after hour as people related their pain and anguish of living under one of the most tyrannical dictators in Europe, a ruler whom even Stalin is said to have urged to ease up on his people. After one visit during which someone again asked the "Why?" question with many tears, I left frustrated. As I walked through the doorway to leave, I breathed a quick request. "O Lord, one day I would like to write a book to help people understand all this." Then I immediately forgot my prayer. But God, it seems, had not.

As I said, I never really intended to prepare such a book. In one sense, perhaps, studying suffering is not possible anyway. Life has to be lived, and it is very hard to share meaningfully with others what you have never experienced yourself. Otherwise we are apt to make truth sound tedious, boring, or even untrue. So what you will find within the following pages is the consequence of a journey. Almost every text and quotation used has been discovered, seemingly accidentally, along the path of real life. So in one sense, this is my spiritual autobiography.

Throughout this book I have consciously tried to be as open and honest as possible. As Christians, and particularly as Christian leaders, we may inadvertently give the impression that we have somehow mastered Christianity. A friend was sharing a problem he was struggling with, and I responded by explaining how I had wrestled with the same issue. He instantly blurted out in astonishment, "What? But you're a pastor! I thought you had it all figured out!"

It's easy to sit discussing deep theological issues and coming up with all sorts of good answers; it's quite another thing to apply what we learn. Sometimes we succeed, but many times we find ourselves cycling through the process of failure and starting out again.

Like my friend, I may watch Christian leaders or others at church from a distance and think that they appear so close to God that they probably don't have any problems as I do. The temptation is to conclude that I struggle alone. But that is not true. We are all struggling in one way or another, because all of us will walk through crucibles—it's just that some of us hide the pain better than others. Perhaps if we were a little more honest about the pain we experience and about our struggles with applying God's teachings to our lives, we would all be stronger for it.

You will notice that I have used a number of fairly long quotations. I have included them in full because they were ones that really helped me. Many of them come from the writings of Ellen White, which God particularly used to encourage me, so I am passing them on as a help to you as well.

Finally, I want to make it clear that I do not consider this book to be the final word on the purpose of suffering. Certainly not. Nor will you find it the most articulate book on the subject, for many great Christians have written more comprehensively and with deeper insight than I have. However, as I noted at the beginning, what I want to try to offer to you is a series of personal insights and lessons that God has taught me. They have been very helpful in providing a way to interpret life and the difficult things I face. Along the way, I have received great encouragement, particularly concerning how God takes difficult situations and uses them to mature His character within us. What matters most to me now is to pass on any encouragement I may have found, because we all face tough times and wonder what to do with them.

So I feel very much like Paul when he wrote, "Praise be to the God and Father of our Lord Jesus Christ, the Father of compassion and the God of all comfort, who comforts us in all our troubles, so that we can comfort those in any trouble with the comfort we ourselves have received from God" (2 Cor. 1:3, 4).

My hope is that all of us may become reservoirs of God's comfort. So when those around us begin to stumble and consider giving up, encouragement will never be far away.

GAVIN ANTHONY
Reykjavik, 2007

CHAPTER 1

Overview of the Journey

"He guides me in paths of righteousness for his name's sake."
Psalm 23:3

We sat across the table from each other sipping chamomile tea, but it was not an ordinary day. Tears flowed freely down her wrinkled cheeks, and her pain and anger was obvious. As she got to the end of her story she asked me, "So where was God? Where was God!"

As I sat there stunned I didn't really know what to say. My degree in theology hadn't quite prepared me for this, and I wasn't sure what if anything could have.

The story I had listened to was filled with anguish and tragedy. Many years before, she had been living in the southern part of Albania as the Communists had begun to take control. Realizing the implications for her family, she had made plans to escape across the border into Greece. Telling only those in her Bible study group, she along with her husband and two children made a midnight trek to the border. But to their astonishment, just as they were nearing the border, waiting soldiers sprang a trap. Someone in their Bible study group was an informer.

The authorities took her young son and daughter away from her and sent both her and her husband to a labor camp. The sentence was particularly hard on her husband. Every time that he refused to work on the Sabbath he received a beating. Eventually he died of the abuse and the exhausting work.

The stress on her two children was overwhelming. They would come and talk to their mother at the prison through the wire fence. It broke her heart to see them standing there barefoot, denied shoes because of the "crimes" of their parents.

The mother had her own traumas. For a period of 18 months the prison authorities kept her in a metal box, one meter square, too small for her ever to lie down in. She remained there through the bitter cold of winter and the stifling heat of summer.

Eventually the government released her, but now she was an enemy of the state. The authorities refused her a place to live and forbade anyone to help her.

And here we were, more than 40 years later, sipping chamomile tea together. I was a young twentysomething free Westerner who had just flown in to help out for a few months now that the Communist dictatorship had finally collapsed. And then I would be leaving. But she, and her questions, would be staying.

So while she was suffering, where was God, and what was He doing?

To be honest, I felt like a fraud trying to answer her question. I could describe a little bit of theory from the Bible, but who was I to explain why she had been hurting so intensely, for so many different reasons, for so many years? What did I know about suffering?

While her question was still hanging in the air, I prayed. Oh how I prayed. I desperately needed something to bring comfort to her.

To be honest, I can't remember exactly what I said, but as I finished, she reached across the table and squeezed my hand, then smiled.

"Thank you," she said with a nod.

She's not the only one to have asked this question. I have raised it myself, and I'm sure you have too. We may not have suffered as she did, but at some point in our lives, with a deep ache in our hearts, we all have cried out, "Where are You?"

Grasping for the Bigger Picture

The problem is that when our hearts are breaking, it's hard to think clearly enough to make sense of what we're enduring, to understand somehow how our personal pain fits into the larger scheme of things.

I know it was about 10 years after my visit to that heartbroken Albanian woman that I began to grasp a sense of a bigger picture that I had not noticed before.

I was on study leave abroad when a friend called my cell phone with some bitter news. Hurrying back to my room, I closed the door and leaned back against it. As the news sank in, I slid onto the floor. The report confirmed something that I had been fearing. Someone that I had considered a friend and a support in my work was spreading very unpleasant gossip about me. What he was saying was not just unkind but intentionally poisonous. It hurt me so much that I hardly knew how to respond. I just couldn't understand how anyone could say such things. Especially someone whom I had thought a friend.

After some time I pulled my Bible off my bed and opened it. Trying to focus through the tears, my eyes finally fixed on some familiar words: "He guides me in paths of righteousness for his name's sake. Even though I walk through the valley of the shadow of death" (Ps. 23:3, 4).

"Even though I walk through the valley of the shadow of death." Yes, it certainly felt like that. But suddenly my gaze jumped back to the previous text: "He guides me in paths of righteousness . . ." My eyes widened quickly. Could it be that this path of righteousness actually passes through the valley of the shadow of death? Could going through the valley of the shadow of death also be "for his name's sake"? I stared, frowning at the text. As I thought about it, I slowly began to view Psalm 23 in a totally new light.

Now, I could see how the paths of righteousness wind their way through green pastures and along quiet waters, but are they still paths of righteousness when we find ourselves in the dark and exposed to our enemies? Could it also be God's design that sometimes He will permit us to experience severe trials, even to lead us into them, "for his name's sake"? It began to dawn on me that perhaps it was possible for the path of righteousness to still be that even when it went down into the valley of shadows.

The Journey of Psalm 23

Before we explore suffering more closely in later chapters, let's first stand back and look at the larger context of suffering as seen through the lens of Psalm 23.

Imagine a picture. All across the canvas in front of us we notice a series of paths—the small, narrow kind that sheep use. They begin on the left-hand side of the canvas, but then twist and turn, going upward, downward, crisscrossing every now and again, before they all finally merge together on our far right. There they become a single path that leads right up to a very large door on the front of a very large house—the house of the Lord (Ps. 23:6).

The house of the Lord is where we are all headed. In the original context the house of the Lord was the Temple where God's people went to worship Him. Of course, we can have intimate communion with God and worship Him now, but we are still on a journey to meet Him in His heavenly temple.

We must always keep in mind that we are not yet there, but we are beginning to walk this path.

Now let's fill in some details from the psalm. The Shepherd (verse 1) stands to the far left, watching over the paths and the sheep that follow them.

Along the paths we see some beautiful lush green pastures (verse 2). Some of the sheep are enjoying a feast.

A little further along the paths we notice some quiet pools of water (verse 2). The Shepherd has already dammed up the stream so that the water is still enough for the sheep to be able to pluck up courage to drink. It is because of the grass and the fresh water that some sheep are feeling totally refreshed and at peace (verse 3).

However, further ahead there looms a very large and dark valley (verse 4). Some of the sheep have already found themselves surrounded by its high walls that seem to block out almost all the light. It looks an evil and terrifying place.

Further down some of the paths we notice what look like picnic tables (verse 5). The Shepherd must have walked ahead and been here earlier too, because He has covered the tables with as much food as the hungry sheep could possibly need. But while some of the sheep are feasting there, enemies lurk nearby. Extremely hungry wolves totally surround the tables, outnumbering the sheep (verse 5).

If you stand back a moment from your painting, you will clearly see that Psalm 23 is a journey. The sheep don't stay in one place all the time, but are moving, always continuing toward the Shepherd's house.

Thus Psalm 23 is a picture of life. It is a depiction both of God's care and of the unexpected. Although the Shepherd provides everything His sheep need (as we can easily see), they will regularly find themselves in unpleasant, difficult, and painful places, ones that they would never choose to be in themselves.

Tips for Surviving the Journey

So how do we prepare for the unexpected? Of course, the simple answer is that we can't completely—otherwise it would not be unexpected. But what we can do is allow Psalm 23 to reshape our perspective on life. So when the unexpected does happen, we will have some idea of how to keep going until we arrive with thanksgiving at the Shepherd's front door.

1. No matter how unprepared and weak we might feel on our journey, the Shepherd promises to provide everything we need.

"The Lord is my shepherd, I shall not be in want" (verse 1).

I remember reading that verse one day and blurting out loud to God, somewhat agitated, "But I do want—I *do* want!"

Here is our first challenge for the journey: if we are to travel without complaining against the Shepherd, we have to accept the fact that our expectations of the journey will start out very different from His. The first obstacle we face is learning to relinquish our escalating demands, expectations, and ambitions for ourselves, and then learning to accept that what God provides is all, and everything, that we need.

2. No matter how bewildering or confusing our journey might be, walking the Shepherd's paths will always accomplish His purposes for our lives.

"He guides me in paths of righteousness for his name's sake" (verse 3).

Notice how Scripture calls all of them "paths of righteousness" (NIV) or "right paths" (NRSV). But why does it refer to them as right or righteous paths?

First, they are right paths because they lead to the right place, the Shepherd's home.

Second, they are right paths because they keep us on a journey in the company of the right person, the Shepherd.

And third, they are right paths because they shape us into the right people. Notice how we travel the paths of righteousness "for his name's sake" (verse 3). "For his name's sake" means for the honor and glory of the Shepherd.

But exactly how do we honor and glorify the Shepherd? We don't honor Him simply by surviving long enough to get to His house without giving up. To become the right people is to live out the purposes of the Shepherd. As we shall increasingly see, we honor the Shepherd most by reflecting His character, and the strange truth is that the Shepherd may accomplish this in us most through permitting us to suffer.

We find this last idea further expanded in the next point.

3. No matter how frightening our journey might be, the darkness is not a place to fear, for it is something that the Shepherd uses to mature us.

"Even though I walk through the valley of the shadow of death, I will fear no evil, for you are with me; your rod and your staff, they comfort me" (verse 4).

When we cannot see the Shepherd because the darkness is so thick, Satan will tempt us to believe that God has abandoned us or that we have taken the wrong route. The reality is the opposite, as Elisabeth Elliot explains: "A lamb who found himself in the valley of the shadow of death might conclude that he had been falsely led. It was needful for him to traverse that darkness in order to learn not to fear. The shepherd is still with him" (Elisabeth Elliot, *Quest for Love* [Grand Rapids: Fleming H. Revell, 1996], p. 218).

Indeed, in the darkness as our enemies endeavor to spring a surprise attack, we suddenly glimpse flashes of our Shepherd at work, beating back our enemies with His rod. And as we sometimes wander off blindly by ourselves and find ourselves so terribly alone and frightened by the sounds in the dark and what we imagine to be out there, we feel the unexpected, and sometimes painful, grip of a shepherd's staff hauling us back to safety.

In those dark valleys, perhaps more than anywhere else, we experience the salvation of the Shepherd and thus we develop confidence in His care.

4. No matter how easy we expect our journey should be, the Shepherd may regularly allow our enemies to surround us in order for us to gain a deeper understanding of His love for us.

"You prepare a table before me in the presence of my enemies. You anoint my head with oil; my cup overflows" (verse 5).

"What would you be thinking," I asked the children at church, "if you had a table with everything you could possibly want on it, but your enemies were standing nearby?"

"I think my enemies would want to steal it all!" chipped in one little boy. He was right! How many times we find ourselves concerned that our enemies are going to rob us of our happiness, our jobs, or God's purposes for us? That is one of the lessons of the table. God places it even under the noses of our enemies, enabling us to realize that nothing they can do will ever take away what He has promised us.

When we see how abundant His blessings are for us, and how nothing and no one can prevent us from receiving them, we find ourselves filled with a renewed wonder and thankfulness at the goodness of our Father. Then we can declare with the psalmist, "I will exalt you, O Lord, for you lifted me out of the depths and did not let my enemies gloat over me" (Ps. 30:1).

5. No matter how lonely our journey might appear to be, the Shepherd is always present.

"Surely goodness and love will follow me all the days of my life, and I will dwell in the house of the Lord forever" (Ps. 23:6).

Both goodness and love are divine attributes. So to be followed by goodness and love is to be followed by God Himself. As David assures us here, goodness and love follows him every single day, not only through the fields of green grass, but also right into the dark valleys. Whether or not the Shepherd has led him into the darkness or whether David has charged off on his own, goodness and love still accompany him. And when his enemies mock him, goodness and love still provide his every need.

Goodness and love never leave him. The Shepherd, Emmanuel, will be with him, even to the very end of the world. And so it is with us.

The Key to Suffering

In her writings Ellen White comments extensively on suffering. In this passage she summarizes much of what we have noticed in Psalm 23 regarding the journey we are on: "Those who are finally victorious will have seasons of terrible perplexity and trial in their religious life; but they must not cast away their confidence, for this is part of their discipline in the school of Christ, and it is essential in order that all the dross may be purged away. The servant of God must endure with fortitude the attacks of the enemy, his grievous taunts, and must overcome the obstacles which Satan will place in his way. . . . But if you keep looking up, not down at your difficulties, you will not faint in the way, you will soon see Jesus reaching His hand to help you, and you will only have to give Him your hand in simple confidence, and let Him lead you. As you become trustful, you will become hopeful. . . . You will find help in Christ to form a strong, symmetrical, beautiful character. Satan cannot make of none effect the light shining forth from such a character. . . . God has given us His best gift, even His only-begotten Son, to uplift, ennoble, and fit us, by putting on us His own perfection of character, for a home in His kingdom" (Ellen G. White, *Messages to Young People* [Nashville: Southern Pub. Assn., 1930], pp. 63, 64).

As we have already begun to notice here and in Psalm 23, the key to understanding suffering is to recognize that suffering is a key. God often permits suffering in our lives because He has the ability to use it as an agent of transformation that enables us to become increasingly similar to the people He originally created in Eden. But this process of God's work in our lives does not happen in a day. It lasts a lifetime.

Joseph: Suffering Transformed

Joseph endured such a process (Gen. 37-50). In three distinctive periods spanning 13 years of unexpected suffering—through family rejection, slavery, and prison—God worked to transform him. The Bible does not give much indication of how Joseph felt during this time, but in the following comments from Ellen White, notice how God is always working to use the situation for unbelievable good. This good was not just for

Joseph, but for the entire ancient Near East, thus shaping the whole future of God's people.

Period 1: God transforms family hatred and rejection into a school to equip a future prime minister with the character he must have to accomplish his role.

When Joseph was 17 God sent him two dreams. The moment he shared those divinely given dreams with his closest family members, his brothers' hatred toward him intensified. When the opportunity arose, they made plans to kill him, but then decided to take the less-painful route by selling him to a caravan of Ishmaelite traders, and made some pocket money as a bonus.

When his brothers first rejected him, Ellen White notes that "for a time Joseph gave himself up to uncontrolled grief and terror.

"But, in the providence of God, even this experience was to be a blessing to him" (Ellen G. White, *Patriarchs and Prophets* [Mountain View, Calif.: Pacific Press Pub. Assn., 1890], p. 213).

Yet as he reflected on his life, a new determination filled him. "His soul thrilled with the high resolve to prove himself true to God—under all circumstances to act as became a subject of the King of heaven. He would serve the Lord with undivided heart; he would meet the trials of his lot with fortitude and perform every duty with fidelity" (*ibid.*, p. 214).

Period 2: God transforms slavery in Egypt into a school to equip a future prime minister with diplomatic skills.

For 10 years Joseph remained a slave. He had no contact with his family, and his father believed him to be dead.

Joseph could have found lots of good reasons to become depressed working so long as a slave. But he did not give in to bitterness. Ellen White comments that "Joseph's gentleness and fidelity won the heart of the chief captain, who came to regard him as a son rather than a slave. The youth was brought in contact with men of rank and learning, and he acquired a knowledge of science, of languages, and of affairs—an education needful to the future prime minister of Egypt" (*ibid.*, p. 217).

Period 3: God transforms false accusation and prison into a school to teach a future prime minister wise leadership.

The next three years Joseph spent in prison because his master's wife falsely accused him of attempted rape. To add insult to injury, someone he had encouraged in prison and who promised to return the favor forgot his promise.

Joseph's attitude under pressure was remarkable, and the consequences far-reaching. "He found a work to do, even in the prison. God was preparing him in the school of affliction for greater usefulness, and he did not refuse the needful discipline. In the prison, witnessing the results of oppression and tyranny and the effects of crime, he learned lessons of justice, sympathy, and mercy, that prepared him to exercise power with wisdom and compassion" (*ibid.*, p. 218).

During his time of great suffering, do you think Joseph had any clue about what God was doing in his life, or could see any evidence that his pain would eventually serve a greater good? I doubt it. But throughout the process he trusted his heavenly Father.

Always for Good
Like Joseph, those who have been closest to God have often suffered the most. Could anyone have been closer to the Father than Jesus, yet has anyone suffered more? David, Moses, Abraham, Paul, and the disciples all endured much, but as the years of their journey rolled by, God demonstrated again and again that indeed "all things work together for good to those who love God, to those who are the called according to His purposes" (Rom. 8:28, NKJV).

The good news is that His purposes are just as good and as noble for us as they were for His people in Bible times, and the transformational blessings He wishes to pour through us are just as great.

God's work in us is the journey of a lifetime. It is often unexpected, sometimes painful, but always under the guidance of a loving Shepherd, and always, always, for good.

Father,
> *Thank You that I do not walk alone.*
> *Thank You that are with me, in the dark as well as in the light.*
> *Thank You also that the path we tread is for Your glory.*
> *May the pursuit of Your glory grow in importance and value within my life.*
In Jesus' name, amen.

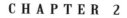

CHAPTER 2

Don't Be Surprised by the Crucibles!

"Dear friends, do not be surprised at the painful trial you are suffering, as though something strange were happening to you."
1 Peter 4:12

In the first chapter we looked at the big picture of our journey to the Shepherd's house. We saw how the path of righteousness involved both good and hard experiences. Now we will sharpen the focus on the times during this journey that we go through the tough times that cause us heartache.

Perhaps you remember using a crucible in science classes at school? It was a small, shallow, metal dish that I remember balancing on top of a black metal tripod. Underneath it we fired up a Bunsen burner with its fierce flame that we aimed at the bottom of the dish. Into the dish we placed various materials that quickly began to heat up, and then we all stood around in small groups with goggles protecting our eyes as we watched to see what would happen. As the dish became hotter, the materials inside began to melt, fizzle, spit, or burn brightly.

Merriam-Webster's Collegiate Dictionary defines a crucible as:

"1. a vessel of a very refractory material (as porcelain) used for melting and calcining a substance that requires a high degree of heat.

"2. a severe test.

"3. a place or situation in which concentrated forces interact to cause or influence change or development."

We could consider the times that we experience trials as crucibles. It is also possible to have spiritual crucibles in our journey with God in which His tests feel heavy and severe and we don't know how to respond. Circumstances seem to conspire against us and threaten to change the way things have always been. None of these experiences may feel pleasant, and more often than not, they take us completely by surprise.

The Problem of Surprise

An interesting poem expresses this inner struggle and surprise in coming to terms with suffering that happens under the watching eye of God. As you read the poem, listen to the poet's surprise and disbelief echoing through the verses:

> "Is it true, O Christ in Heaven,
> That the highest suffer most?
> That the strongest wander furthest,
> And more helplessly are lost?
> That the mark of rank in nature
> Is capacity for pain?
> And the anguish of the singer
> Makes the sweetness of the strain?
>
> "Is it true, O Christ in Heaven,
> That whichever way we go
> Walls of darkness must surround us,
> Things we would but cannot know?
> That the infinite must bound us
> Like a temple veil unrent,
> Whilst the finite ever wearies,
> So that none's therein content?"

Don't Be Surprised, Because . . .

Peter urges us all, "Dear friends, do not be surprised at the painful trial you are suffering, as though something strange were happening to you" (1 Peter 4:12). The apostle is writing to people who were suffering for being Christians, but I believe that what he is saying applies to all types of suffering. No suffering should surprise us.

The Greek word for "surprised" means to be "alien" or "foreign." Peter here urges his readers not to fall into the trap of believing that fiery ordeals and trials are alien to Christian experience. They are not aberrations to Christian living, but should be considered a normal part of it. They must be expected. The word used for "fiery ordeal" (NRSV) or "painful trial" (NIV) or "fiery trial" (NKJV), comes from another Greek word that means "a burning." In other places it is translated "furnace." We could consider the experience of suffering for our faith as a "smelting process" (Kenneth S. Wuest, *Wuest's Word Studies From the Greek New Testament* [Grand Rapids: Eerdmans, 1997]), the experience of the crucible.

Jesus emphasized the same thing as His disciples huddled around to hear Him explain about the end of the world. "You will hear of wars and rumors of wars" He said, "but see to it that you are not alarmed. Such things must happen" (Matt. 24:6).

So we are not to be surprised. Let's now look in detail at why we shouldn't be. Here are four biblical reasons we should expect to experience pain and suffering, even though all we want to do is live a life that pleases God.

1. Don't be surprised at suffering, because Satan is at work in our world. "But terror will come on the earth and the sea. For the Devil has come down to you in great anger, and he knows that he has little time" (Rev. 12:12, NLT).

Yesterday was another ordinary day. Like all the other people in my town, I got in my car and drove to work. But as I turned on the radio and began listening to the news, I couldn't believe what the BBC reporter was saying. Far away in northern Uganda, far away from anything that has got anything to do with me, some doctors were trying to restore the faces of young girls who had had their noses and ears cut off by rebel soldiers, soldiers who were hardly into their teens.

I felt sick. In spite of the reported success of the operations, it all seemed so irrelevant. I called out aloud in my car like Habakkuk, "How long, O God? How long can You look at all this and not intervene?"

That was yesterday. As I said, it was an ordinary day. It was perhaps not like the not-so-ordinary days when terrorists destroyed the twin towers in New York or the Asian tsunami killed more than 300,000 people in multiple countries.

But I don't need to hear about Uganda, Asia, or the United States, which are all thousands of miles away from where I sit. Four miles from where I was living, a 13-year-old boy in a quiet English village broke into the house of an 80-year-old woman and raped her.

Satan is very much active in the physical world, but he works perhaps even more powerfully and painfully through people. If possible, he will use gossip and criticism daintily dropped into our ears in an effort to cause tension, hurt, discouragement, and friction.

So how do we respond? Peter urges us, "Be self-controlled and alert. Your enemy the devil prowls around like a roaring lion looking for someone to devour. Resist him, standing firm in the faith, because you know that your brothers throughout the world are undergoing the same kind of sufferings" (1 Peter 5:8, 9).

Notice in these verses four characteristics we need to practice.

First, be self-controlled. Don't allow the pressures that Satan creates around us to shape our thoughts, feelings, and actions. Second, be alert. We must keep our eyes open and watching so that we never forget who is really at work. Third, we must resist, refusing to give in or become overwhelmed by the pressure Satan that brings. God is still on our side! Fourth, stand firm in the faith. This builds on the idea of resisting but identifies that our standing firm is grounded in our faith. Faith is what keeps us from buckling under Satan's attacks.

Peter assures the believers that though they may struggle for a while, God offers them a promise: "And the God of all grace, who called you to his eternal glory in Christ, after you have suffered a little while, will himself restore you and make you strong, firm and steadfast" (verse 10). And that's a promise for us too.

2. Don't be surprised at suffering that results from reaping the consequences of our own sin. "For the wages of sin is death" (Rom. 6:23).

We also experience heartache because we do foolish and sinful things. As Paul says, "the wages of sin is death." Born as sinful beings into a sinful world, we are unavoidably on the path to a literal death. But our choices to sin against God bring with them spiritual and eternal death also. And we will surely suffer for such decisions today.

If I am rude to people, they will start avoiding me. Should I sleep around, I risk catching sexually transmitted diseases and the emotional and spiritual distress that goes with them. And if I choose to ignore the Holy Spirit's guidance, I will walk this life powerless and alone.

In Romans 1:18-32 Paul describes this sort of suffering as the result of God's wrath. Here in this context the wrath of God is simply the consequences we experience from rejecting Him. Paul first establishes that because of what God has created, every human being has no excuse to be ignorant that He exists and what sort of deity He is. The apostle claims that to ignore this in the face of the facts is willful sin that has terrible consequences. For after each step of rejecting God, we will find ourselves deeper in sin and therefore in its pain.

The first step away from Him is deliberately refusing to honor Him. The consequence for those who knowingly turn from God? "Their thinking became futile and their foolish hearts were darkened" (verse 21).

The second step away from the Lord results from making substitutes for Him, especially in the form of idols. "Therefore God gave them over in the sinful desires of their hearts to sexual impurity for the degrading of their bodies with one another" (verse 24).

The third step involves creating substitutes for all of God's truth and then wholeheartedly worshipping such human inventions. "Because of this, God gave them over to shameful lusts. Even their women exchanged natural relations for unnatural ones. In the same way the men also abandoned natural relations with women and were inflamed with lust for one another. Men committed indecent acts with other men, and received in themselves the due penalty for their perversion" (verses 26, 27).

The fourth and final step occurs when human beings completely reject the knowledge of God. The consequence for them is that God "gave them over to a depraved mind, to do what ought not to be done. . . . They are full of envy, murder, strife, deceit and malice. They are gossips, slanderers, God-haters, insolent, arrogant and boastful; they invent ways of doing evil; they disobey their parents" (verses 28-30).

Notice that as we increasingly cut off our vertical relationship with God, we have growing problems in our horizontal relationships with our fellow human beings. More important, it is the sexual problems that Paul highlights, in which we become impure (step 2), then perverted (step 3), until our minds, the place where we control ourselves, are unrecoverable (step 4). The struggles and perversion of sexuality in our culture today is a primary symptom of our drift from God.

How do we reverse this downward tendency to death? The answer is not complicated. We have to choose again for God alone and allow the principles of His kingdom to shape our values and beliefs. As we struggle with the pressures of turbulent and seductive feelings, we have to ask for a willing heart and mind that will allow His power will bring us new life.

"You see, at just the right time, when we were still powerless, Christ died for the ungodly" (Rom. 5:6). "And if the Spirit of him who raised Jesus from the dead is living in you, he who raised Christ from the dead will also give life to your mortal bodies through his Spirit, who lives in you" (Rom. 8:11). Out of the crucible of suffering for our sin, God can always bring new life, and therefore, we always have hope.

Suffering in the Lives of Christians

We have just covered the first two reasons we should not be surprised at suffering. From the Christian's point of view, they may appear obvious. But there are other reasons for suffering that may surprise us and that we may even find hard to recognize.

A friend voiced such surprise as we walked together. The tropical air was pleasant and warm, but the conversation was tense.

"But why?" he questioned with astonishment. "Why is all this happening to us?"

He was searching for sensible answers, but nothing sounded satisfactory. Why should he and his family be suffering so much hatred and backstabbing when all they wanted to do was serve God? After months of anguish, he now had to cope with having all of his good intentions being misrepresented and taken out of context. Events were shredding his reputation.

"How can God allow this?" he continued. "Can't He see that I am simply trying to do my best?" After some months without relief, he quit his job, and he and his family flew home.

I remember driving back to the airport after my short visit. I could hardly speak. They were a good Christian family—in my opinion, doing a great job, but being crushed by what seemed to be overwhelming pressure. Even now as I write and remember the shattered hopes and disillusionment of so many people, I can't help feeling deeply sad.

But even as Christians, should we be surprised? As we have already noted, Satan is at work in the world and he normally operates through people in his efforts to cause pain. So let's go on to examine why God may allow suffering to persist, particularly in the lives of Christians, for these reasons will become the main focus of the book.

3. Don't be surprised at suffering if God is in the process of purifying your life from sin. "Therefore this is what the Lord Almighty says: 'See, I will refine and test them, for what else can I do because of the sin of my people?'" (Jer. 9:7).

Even though we may have deliberately sinned, we remain precious to God. So during His efforts to make us pure and blameless like Him (Rev. 14:5), He may risk us feeling extremely hurt as He takes out His scalpel and, like a surgeon, begins to cut into the sin that has entwined itself in the very depths of our beings. And when this happens, it is rarely done under anesthetic, for God wants us to understand the terrible consequences of our actions.

In Jeremiah 9 the prophet continues to announce God's plans for the refinement of His people. "Therefore, this is what the Lord Almighty, the God of Israel, says: 'See, I will make this people eat bitter food and drink poisoned water. I will scatter them among nations that neither they nor their fathers have known'" (verses 15, 16). When we read such passages, we may be tempted to misunderstand God. But as we shall continue to see in the following chapters, He employs such methods not because He delights in our pain, but because He longs so much for our holiness.

Oswald Chambers describes this work rather bluntly: "Jesus Christ had not tenderness whatever toward anything that is ultimately going to ruin a man in the service of God. . . . If the Spirit of God brings to your mind a word of the Lord that hurts you, you may be sure that there is something He wants to hurt to death" (*My Utmost for His Highest* [Uhrichsville, Ohio: Barbour and Co., Inc., 1963], reading for Sept. 27).

And God may persevere in such a refining process for a long time. "God has shown me that He gave His people a bitter cup to drink, to purify and cleanse them. It is a bitter draught, and they can make it still more bitter by murmuring, complaining, and repining. But those who receive it thus must have another draught, for the first does not have its designed effect upon the heart. And if the second does not effect the work, then they must have another, and another, until it does have its designed effect, or they will be left filthy, impure in heart. I saw that this bitter cup can be sweetened by patience, endurance, and prayer, and that it will have its designed effect upon the hearts of those who thus receive it, and God will be honored and glorified" (Ellen G. White, *Early Writings* [Washington, D.C.: Review and Herald Publishing Association, 1945], p. 47).

God longs for us to be pure. Malachi reflects on this high purpose: "He will sit as a refiner and purifier of silver; he will purify the Levites and refine them like gold and silver. Then the Lord will have men who will bring offerings in righteousness" (Mal. 3:3).

So we shouldn't be surprised at the pain of this crucible and shouldn't be discouraged. God still has plans for us. Reflecting the righteousness of our Father is what such crucibles of purification are all about.

4. Don't be surprised at suffering if God is pruning you to grow increasingly fruitful. "He cuts off every branch in me that bears no fruit, while every branch that does bear fruit he prunes so that it will be even more fruitful" (John 15:2).

The painful pruning process illustrated in John 15:1-5 is extremely vital for the maturing Christian. We may not have sinned in a specific way that we can think of, but as sinners, we know that we are still weak in our faith and trust. And all the other spiritual graces that God longs to fill us with will be limited in quality and strength.

In his helpful little book *Secrets of the Vine* Bruce Wilkinson identifies a strange paradox: "Are you praying for God's superabundant blessings and pleading that He will make you more like His Son? If so, then you are asking for the shears" (Sisters, Oreg.: Multnomah Publishers, Inc., 2001, p. 60).

I was explaining to a woman this idea that God Himself sometimes leads us into difficult and painful situations to refine us. Staring at me in horror, she exclaimed, "I can't believe God could do something like that!" She fully thought that I was disparaging God's character.

So does God cause us to experience pain?

Charles Stanley replies, "The comfortable, but theologically incorrect, answer is no. You will find many people preaching and teaching that God never sends an ill wind into a person's life, but that position can't be justified by Scripture. The Bible teaches that God does send adversity—but within certain parameters and always for a reason that relates to our growth, perfection, and eternal good" (*Advancing Through Adversity,* electronic ed. [Nashville: Thomas Nelson, 1997]).

Consider Paul. "To keep me from becoming conceited because of these surpassingly great revelations," he wrote, "there was given me a thorn in my flesh, a messenger of Satan, to torment me. Three times I pleaded with the Lord to take it away from me" (2 Cor. 12:7, 8). Notice that the apostle considers that he was "given" this painful "thorn." He regards it as "a messenger of Satan," yet he sees that it was intended for a holy purpose, for God permits the thorn to keep him humble.

But what was it? Ellen White says it was bad eyesight. "He [Paul] was ever to carry about with him in the body the marks of Christ's glory, in his eyes, which had been blinded by the heavenly light" (*The Seventh-day Adventist Bible Commentary*, Ellen G. White Comments, vol. 6, p. 1058). In the same way that Jacob fought with Jesus and received a blessing, yet continued to have a limp from the encounter (Gen. 32:31), Paul carried a constant reminder that unless he could see Christ clearly, he and those he ministered to would remain in spiritual darkness. God permitted a physical problem to remain in the apostle for a spiritual benefit.

As far as I am concerned this has been true for me. Since I was 27 I have had to use a pacemaker, because my heart is weak. During the years since then, the overwhelming lesson that God has been teaching me is total dependence on His power alone in my work for Him. I am personally convinced that while God could have healed me permanently, He has allowed this physical problem to remain in order to emphasize this spiritual lesson. For without my external power source, I am nothing.

So when God allows us to experience crucibles of maturing, it is good to remember His promise to Paul: "My grace is sufficient for you, for my power is made perfect in weakness" (2 Cor. 12:9).

Ellen White alludes to these strange providences of God for our maturing. "He who reads the hearts of men knows their characters better than they themselves know them. He sees that some have powers and susceptibilities which, rightly directed, might be used in the advancement of His work. In His providence He brings these persons into different positions and varied circumstances that they may discover in their character the defects which have been concealed from their own knowledge. He gives them opportunity to correct these defects and to fit themselves for His service. Often He permits the fires of affliction to assail them that they may be purified" (*The Ministry of Healing* [Mountain View, Calif.: Pacific Press Pub. Assn., 1905], p. 471).

So it's not necessarily that we have done something wrong when we find ourselves in the Father's crucibles, but that we are weak, and God wants us to blossom and mature beyond our wildest dreams.

Putting It Together

As we have seen, crucibles can come into our lives for very different reasons. We do not have space to cover all of them, but as we continue, we are going to focus on the particular crucibles that God uses to enable us to become more useful to Him and His kingdom. For the Christian, life will inevitably include them. Charles Swindoll leaves us with no doubt: "Someone put it this way, 'Whoever desires to walk with God walks right into the crucible.' All who choose godliness live in a crucible. The tests will come" (*Moses, Great Lives From God's Word* [Nashville: Word Pub. Co., 1999], p. 285).

Our challenge is that when those tests do arrive, we will not be tempted to crumple and to lose our hope. How we can learn to do this is what the rest of the book is about.

Father,
I am fearful and unsure about the thought of heartache being part of Your holy purpose.
It appears such a contradiction of everything.
Open my eyes to understand Your purposes and Your methods.
And grant me the courage to follow You,
No matter the cost.
In Jesus' name, amen.

CHAPTER 3

Case Studies in the Crucible: Watching God at Work

"By day the Lord went ahead of them in a
pillar of cloud to guide them on their way . . ."
Exodus 13:21

In C. S. Lewis' famous book *The Lion, the Witch and the Wardrobe,* Mr. Badger tells the children—recently fallen out of the wardrobe into the kingdom of Narnia—about their king, Aslan. To their astonishment, Mr. Badger reveals that his ruler is actually a lion.

"'Ooh!' said Susan, 'I'd thought he was a man. Is he—quite safe? I shall feel nervous about meeting a Lion.'. . .

"'Safe?' said Mr. Beaver. 'Don't you hear what Mrs. Beaver tells you? Who said anything about safe? 'Course he isn't safe. But he's good'" (pp. 75, 76).

Mr. Badger highlights the struggle we face in trying to understand how God can be both good and "unsafe" at the same time. We often feel that in order for Him to be a good deity, He must also be understandable and predictable. In other words, He needs to be "safe."

But as you have probably already discovered, God is not always understandable, and rarely predictable. And it is particularly the case when it comes to His involvement in our suffering.

You may be tempted to interrupt me and argue that suffering is still not part of God's plan for our lives and is certainly not an aspect of His redeeming purposes for us.

But I don't think it's quite as simple as that.

Make sure you are sitting comfortably, because in this chapter we are going to work through some heavy issues together, and you will want to think and reflect slowly as we continue.

Blunt Talk About Painful Discipline

In chapter 1 we considered a general context for suffering through the lens of Psalm 23. Then in chapter 2 we began to focus more closely at four specific reasons for such suffering. In this chapter, and indeed, the rest of the book, we will attempt to unpack and understand those times of suffering that God uses for our spiritual maturing.

That may sound like a contradiction. Should suffering and pain lead to spiritual maturity? And more specifically, does God have any direct involvement in this?

As Psalm 23 gives a general context for suffering in the Christian's life, Hebrews 12 provides an overview of the suffering that God employs for our spiritual development. The book of Hebrews says that this type of suffering is the result of God's "discipline," a word used to explain the teaching or training that God employs for our good.

So let's take a quick tour through Hebrews 12. We're going to consider six principles that begin to provide a framework for understanding the painful discipline that God allows for our spiritual growth.

1. The suffering of a life under God's discipline is never meaningless. Leon Morris notes that while we all suffer and suffering is unpleasant "it is not quite so bad when it can be seen as meaningful" (in *The Expositor's Bible Commentary,* vol. 12, p. 136). Morris then points out that the author of Hebrews has demonstrated that Jesus suffered and persevered because of the great meaning that His suffering would have—the redemption of the world. Indeed because of "the joy set before him [He] endured the cross, scorning its shame, and sat down at the right hand of the throne of God" (Heb. 12:2).

The biblical writer's point should be clear as he turns this idea back onto his readers—to those of us who tend to think that our suffering is random and purposeless and who have perhaps "forgotten that word of encouragement" (verse 5). He charges us all, "Consider him who endured such opposition from sinful men, so that you will not grow weary and lose heart" (verse 3). When things get tough, he points us to Jesus. Christ overcame suffering because of His conviction that when the Father permits such suffering, it is always for God's glory and always for our eternal good. So the biblical writer wants to assure us that our suffering under divine discipline has as much purpose as the suffering in the life of Jesus. So we must not give up just because we can't see the purpose yet!

2. Suffering as a result of God's discipline is an evidence of His closeness to us rather than the result of His abandoning us. "My son, do not make light of the Lord's discipline, and do not lose heart when he rebukes you, because the Lord disciplines those he loves, and he punishes everyone he accepts as a son. . . . For what son is not disciplined by his father? If you are not disciplined (and everyone undergoes discipline), then you are illegitimate children and not true sons. Moreover, we have all had human fathers who disciplined us and we respected them for it. How much more should we submit to the Father of our spirits and live!" (verses 5-9).

The apostle wants to be clear. Of course our Father is going to work with us, train us, and mold us! If He was not concerned about us, He would have lost interest in us a long time ago. However, His personal, yet painful, intervention in our lives is because He is not ready to let us go that easily. He loves us too much to do that.

3. Our ability to mature spiritually under God's discipline depends on how we choose to view our suffering. "Endure hardship as discipline; God is treating you as sons" (verse 7). Notice carefully what the text is saying. When difficulties come, *consider* that you are under divine discipline. In other words, don't moan and groan that life is unfair. It certainly is—because Satan is at work. But because God is still sovereign in the world, we can be certain that He knows about our problems and that He will transform them at the right time. But we have to trust Him in this. It won't work if we drop our faith like a hot brick, then walk around feeling sorry for ourselves.

4. The ultimate purpose of God's discipline is always that we will reflect His character. "Our fathers disciplined us for a little while as they thought best; but God disciplines us for our good, that we may share in his holiness" (verse 10). Our sharing in His own holiness—His character—is the goal. However, if we are going to persevere through such discipleship, the holiness of God must be attractive to us and be completely compelling.

5. There is no shortcut around the pain of God's discipline. I wish this was not true, but at least Scripture is honest about it: "No discipline seems pleasant at the time but painful" (verse 11). We can't avoid the pain from God's discipline. But the pain I feel comes not from Him, but from within me. The pain I experience in God's hands is normally the pain from my reluctance or inability to abandon the sin so deeply rooted inside.

6. The blessings of God's discipline will become noticeable, but not necessarily immediately. "Later on, however, it produces a harvest of righteousness and peace for those who have been trained by it" (verse 11). Notice how the passage places the blessing of righteousness and peace in the future. It assures us that the blessings will come, but not necessarily today. In the meantime, we have to persevere, trusting God without completely understanding Him.

Does God Only "Permit" Suffering?

Let's now take our study a step further. It is one thing to believe that God can use suffering to transform the effects of Satan's activity in our lives. But does the Lord ever deliberately discipline His people by leading them Himself into places that He knows beforehand they will struggle and experience pain?

Ellen White certainly thought so. In the following passage she compares God to the owner of a bird who wants to teach it how to sing. "In the full light of day, and in hearing of the music of other voices, the caged bird will not sing the song that his master seeks to teach him. He learns a snatch of this, a trill of that, but never a separate and entire melody. But the master covers the cage, and places it where the bird will listen to the one song he is to sing. In the dark, he tries and tries again to sing that song until it is learned, and he breaks forth in perfect melody. Then the bird is brought forth, and ever after he can sing that song in the light. Thus God deals with His children. He has a song to teach us, and when we have learned it amid the shadows of affliction we can sing it ever afterward" (*The Ministry of Healing*, p. 472).

Can you trust such an "unsafe" God?

However, you may still be quite wary of the idea that God may act like this Himself. So let's consider four crucibles of God's discipline, into which He personally directed His people.

1. God led Israel into the crucible to mature their knowledge and trust of Him.

When the Israelites escaped from Egypt, do you remember who was leading them at all times? Was it Moses out there at the head of the line? No, it was "the Lord" Himself. Jesus was in the pillar of cloud that directed them. "By day the Lord went ahead of them in a pillar of cloud to guide them on their way and by night in a pillar of fire to give them light, so that they could travel by day or night. Neither the pillar of cloud by day nor the pillar of fire by night left its place in front of the people" (Ex. 13:21, 22).

God is out there guiding His people through the blistering heat. Can you see where He is going? The journey began as Jesus (walking within the cloud, remember?) led His people into a trap—the Red Sea spread out in front, the mountains towering on either side, and the powerful Egyptian army closing in behind. Do you think the people were scared? Absolutely.

"As Pharaoh approached, the Israelites looked up, and there were the Egyptians, marching after them. They were terrified and cried out to the Lord. They said to Moses, 'Was it because there were no graves in Egypt that you brought us to the desert to die? What have you done to us by bringing us out of Egypt? Didn't we say to you in Egypt, "Leave us alone; let us serve the Egyptians"? It would have been better for us to serve the Egyptians than to die in the desert!'" (Ex. 14:10-12).

If God was such a good and loving shepherd, why did He lead them into a situation that He knew would frighten His children? Would you do this to your own children?

Though God's actions caused His people some temporary grief, the benefits to them were worth it. Concerning the newly released slaves, God had promised Moses, "I will harden Pharaoh's heart, and he will pursue them. But I will gain glory for myself through Pharaoh and all his army, and the Egyptians will know that I am the Lord" (verse 4). For His own honor God created a situation in which His salvation would become an international talking point, and His people would reap the rewards. As Rahab told the spies many years later: "We have heard how the Lord dried up the water of the Red Sea for you when you came out of Egypt. . . . When we heard of it, our hearts melted and everyone's courage failed because of you, for the Lord your God is God in heaven above and on the earth below" (Joshua 2:10, 11).

So because of Moses' confidence in God, he replied to the fearful people shaking by the water's edge. "Do not be afraid. Stand firm and you will see the deliverance the Lord will bring you today. The Egyptians you see today you will never see again. The Lord will fight for you; you need only to be still" (Ex. 14:13, 14).

After leaving the Red Sea, the Israelites walked for three waterless days in the baking heat of the desert of Shur, but they did not wander aimlessly, because the Lord was leading them in the pillar of cloud and fire—straight to Marah.

Marah? Didn't God know about the problem with its water supply? Didn't He realize that the situation would severely irritate His children when, hot and thirsty, they discovered only bitter water? And wouldn't that be a completely natural and understandable response for them?

Of course it was. And this natural response was what He was trying to transform. God did this on purpose. As Moses wrote, it was "there he tested them" (Ex. 15:25).

All through the desert and throughout Israel's history God Himself regularly brought His own people to testing crucibles, usually painful, to see if they would trust Him, and learn to feel their need of His great salvation.

2. God led Jesus into the crucible so that He could minister to others. At the very beginning of Jesus' ministry Luke describes how the Holy Spirit directed Him into the desert to face temptation from Satan. "Jesus, full of the Holy Spirit, returned from the Jordan and was led by the Spirit in the desert, where for forty days he was tempted by the devil" (Luke 4:1, 2).

Did the Holy Spirit make a mistake? Didn't He know that Satan was going to spring an ambush?

It was not the only time that Jesus suffered. The author of Hebrews describes how such suffering was necessary for Him to endure in order to accomplish His mission. "During the days of Jesus' life on earth, he offered up prayers and petitions with loud cries and tears to the one who could save him from death" (Heb. 5:7). Isaiah portrays His suffering rather bluntly: "He was oppressed and afflicted, yet he did not open his mouth; he was led like a lamb to the slaughter, and as a sheep before her shearers is silent, so he did not open his mouth. . . . Yet it was the Lord's will to crush him and cause him to suffer" (Isa. 53:7-10).

As the last text infers: "Christ's mission could be fulfilled only through suffering" (Ellen G. White, *The Desire of Ages* [Mountain View, Calif.: Pacific Press Pub. Assn., 1898], p. 129). In the same way, perhaps the mission that God has given us can be accomplished only through suffering also.

It is vital to remember that such suffering in God's hands is not necessarily because we have taken a wrong turn. "We should not lose courage when assailed by temptation. Often when placed in a trying situation we doubt that the Spirit of God has been leading us. But it was the Spirit's leading that brought Jesus into the wilderness to be tempted by Satan. When God brings us into trial, He has a purpose to accomplish for our good" (*ibid.*, p. 126).

3. God led the early church into the crucible to mature its faith. This same testing happened in the early church. Writing to all those scattered across what is today modern Turkey, Peter explains, "These [all kinds of trials] have come so that your faith—of greater worth than gold, which perishes even though refined by fire—may be proved genuine and may result in praise, glory and honour when Jesus Christ is revealed" (1 Peter 1:7).

Notice that he says, "These [trials] have come so that . . ." In the phrase "so that" the apostle recognizes purpose in their suffering. God is not the source of their pain, but He is guiding events to use them for a holy cause.

This purpose focuses on faith. Peter declares that their faith was "of greater worth than gold." Just as fire purifies gold, through suffering their faith would be matured and "be proved genuine." The result of such faith is twofold. Refined faith would keep them strong and courageous, but as the text says, such faith will also result in praise, glory, and honor for Jesus when He "is revealed." Faith matured in the middle of suffering today will result in the universe glorifying Jesus later—at the Second Coming. Imagine Jesus appearing in the clouds and the unfallen beings across the universe singing His praises. They sing because they see rising from the earth those who have faithfully resisted the temptation to buckle and fall under great pressure, and they point to Jesus as the one who has made such a thing possible.

God is looking for genuine faith, but it often comes in the same way as genuine gold. It's made under high pressure, with fire—just as in the crucible.

4. God led the Adventist pioneers into the crucible to purify His people's motives.

The Lord did not abandon this method of testing 2,000 years ago. Was it not God Himself who led the pioneers of the Seventh-day Adventist Church into the deepest disappointment?

Adventists have always seen themselves in the events of Revelation 10:9-11, which we understand to refer to the pioneers' misunderstanding of one of the prophecies in the book of Daniel. Their mistake led to what became known as the Great Disappointment. "So I went to the angel and asked him to give me the little scroll. He said to me, 'Take it and eat it. It will turn your stomach sour, but in your mouth it will be as sweet as honey.' I took the little scroll from the angel's hand and ate it. It tasted as sweet as honey in my mouth, but when I had eaten it, my stomach turned sour. Then I was told, 'You must prophesy again about many peoples, nations, languages and kings.'"

Ellen White describes what happened: "I saw the people of God joyful in expectation, looking for their Lord. But God designed to prove them. His hand covered a mistake in the reckoning of the prophetic periods" (*Early Writings,* p. 235).

It was certainly the pioneers who misinterpreted the prophecies though she describes God as the one prolonging their bewilderment.

Such a thing appears hard to understand, and again shows the risks that God takes in being misunderstood. And He certainly was by some at the time. "In the period of doubt and uncertainty that followed the disappointment, many of the advent believers yielded their faith. Dissensions and divisions came in. The majority opposed with voice and pen the few who, following in the providence of God, received the Sabbath reform and began to proclaim the third angel's message. Many who should have devoted their time and talents to the one purpose of sounding warning to the world were absorbed in opposing the Sabbath truth, and in turn, the labor of its advocates was necessarily spent in answering these opponents and defending the truth. Thus the work was hindered, and the world was left in darkness" (Ellen G. White, *Selected Messages* [Washington, D.C.: Review and Herald Pub. Assn., 1958], book 1, p. 68).

But this crucible achieved its purpose. God had refined His people to determine who was truly committed. The group became fewer but stronger. They were ready to accept the next message from God, which they then eagerly shared with the world.

What About Today?

We have looked briefly at four examples of God's activity in history. But what about today?

It's exactly the same. "But of old the Lord led His people to Rephidim, and He may choose to lead us there also, to test our loyalty. He does not always bring us to pleasant places. If He did, in our self-sufficiency we should forget that He is our helper. He longs to manifest Himself to us, and to reveal the abundant supplies at our disposal, and He permits trial and disappointment to come to us that we may realize our helplessness, and learn to call upon Him for aid. He can cause cooling streams to flow from the flinty rock. We shall never know, until we are face to face with God, when we shall see as we are seen, and know as we are known, how many burdens He has borne for us, and how many burdens He would have been glad to bear, if, with childlike faith, we had brought them to Him" (Ellen G. White, "Rephidim," *Review and Herald,* Apr. 7, 1903).

Hanging On in the Crucible

As we learn to hang on during such experiences, it is helpful to notice a three-step process that often follows affliction in the Shepherd's crucible.

1. Examination. When Israel came to the Red Sea, would they believe that God was still good? that He was still leading? It was the same for those in the Great Disappointment. Many complained against God and refused to go any further, but others still trusted. Will we say, "Though he slay me, yet will I trust in him" (Job. 13:15, KJV), or not? Such times sift our motives and ambitions, and we come to a clearer knowledge of ourselves. It is now that our striving for communion with Him becomes critical to our spiritual survival.

2. Revelation. At Marah God demonstrated His care through the sweetening of the water, and for those early Adventists, there came the recognition that the Lord was still there as He opened their understanding and new and glorious light flooded in. But like Jacob, who hung on for the blessing, it happens only to those who refuse to let go of God. No matter how hard the examination has been, no matter how dark the valley, light will eventually sweep the darkness aside.

3. Reorientation. Here is the crunch point. Will we learn from what God has revealed and alter what we earlier thought to be true? Or will we hang on to our own dreams, our own view of the way that we think life and God should be? Would Israel accept God's care even when things didn't seem to be working out as they thought? Would the early Adventists have the courage to admit their mistake regarding their prophetic calculations and preach on? When the light does arrive, it is a call to adjust ourselves to God's continuing revelation.

We must never give up during such trying times! As George MacDonald concludes: "No words can express how much our world 'owes' to sorrow. Most of the Psalms were conceived in a wilderness. Most of the New Testament was written in a prison. The greatest words of God's Scriptures have all passed through great trials. The greatest prophets have 'learned in suffering what they wrote in their books.' So take comfort, afflicted Christian! When our God is about to make use of a person, He allows them to go through a crucible of fire."

Father,
    Thank You for the assurance of Your presence.
    Teach me how to hang on when things are hard.
    Though I may be tempted to run away from You when things go wrong,
    Keep me safe in Your hands.
In Jesus' name, amen.

CHAPTER 4

Character:
The Crucible's Holy Purpose

"And we, who with unveiled faces all reflect the Lord's glory,
are being transformed into his likeness with ever-increasing glory."
2 Corinthians 3:18

I was talking to a group of pastors about the role of character in the Christian's life when one of them, looking slightly bemused, questioned, "Don't you think that the word 'character' is a bit old-fashioned?"

His comment took me back a bit. I had never thought about character being old-fashioned. For me, the word was just coming into vogue.

During the past few decades a clear understanding of character seems to have drifted from our consciousness and has even become confused. Russell Gough, a professor of ethics and philosophy at Pepperdine University and a chair of the annual White House conference on character building, explains why. He observes that from the time of Heraclitus, Aristotle, and the early Greeks, and across different cultures, the concept of character has remained constant: an interrelated combination of our ethical positions, habits, and virtues (or vices). However, the concept of character began to change in the middle of the twentieth century because of the emergence of psychology as an academic discipline, and the proliferation of books on pop psychology and self-improvement. It has led to an emphasis on "the self," on measurable personality traits, and on self-esteem. Such concepts have gradually replaced the historical and deeply meaningful understanding of character, one that emphasized habits of inner integrity, such as loyalty and respect, for these were much more difficult, if not impossible, to measure scientifically. Gough believes that the trend has stripped the historical concept of character of all its rich significance "to the point where 'character' is now often used as a watered-down synonym for 'personality'" (Russell Gough, *Character Is Destiny* [New York: Random House, 1998], chap. 1).

Gough's book is worth a thoughtful read. But as we move on, I want to point to his writing as an example of a growing desire to see the historical meaning of character reclaimed, because the implications, particularly for the Christian community, are far reaching.

Dallas Willard, another professor of philosophy, and the former director of the School of Philosophy at the University of Southern California, also pushes the concept of character onto the Christian agenda with his book *Renovation of the Heart: Putting on the Character of Christ.* Wherever we seem to look these days, character is making a comeback.

What Is Character?

D. L. Moody famously stated that "character is what you are in the dark." He was echoing the historical view that character is not personality or reputation, but concerns the deeper issues of who and what we are within.

The dictionary describes character in a positive way, as "moral excellence and firmness." This gets rather personal, for I can't consider my "great accomplishments" for God or my "hard work" for the church as a safe place for my ego to rest. It's what I am inside that really matters. As Ellen White emphasizes, it is "the thoughts and feelings combined [that] make up the moral character" (Ellen G. White, *Testimonies for the Church* [Mountain View, Calif.: Pacific Press Pub. Assn., 1948], vol. 5, p. 310).

Such an emphasis on the inner life is not intended to be just a trendy idea. Rather, it seeks to address the original sin problem in human beings. In Genesis God joyfully announced, "Let us make man in our image, in our likeness" (Gen. 1:26). But as Genesis continues to recount, Adam and Eve lost that image—the glory of God. As with God Himself, the glory that surrounded them was merely an outward visible sign of their inner perfection. As they chose to disobey God, the glory around them vanished, and they found themselves with nothing to wear. But it wasn't a wardrobe malfunction. Sin had defaced the character of God deep within.

Thus began humanity's desperate quest for salvation. But it was much more than being saved to a better place. Human beings also needed to have restored what they had lost—the character of their God within.

But where would they find such character?

Searching for Character

Irish missionary Amy Carmichael took a group of children to see a traditional goldsmith at work. In the middle of a charcoal fire rested a curved roof tile. On the tile was a mixture of salt, tamarind fruit, and brick dust, and embedded in the mixture was the gold. As the fire devoured the mixture, the gold became purer. Then the goldsmith took the gold out with tongs and if it was not pure enough, replaced it in the fire with more of the mixture. But each time he did so, he made the heat hotter than before. The children asked him, "How do you know when the gold is pure?"

"When I can see my face in it," he replied (Amy Carmichael, *Learning of God* [London: SPCK, 1983], p. 50).

Here is an image of vivid contrasts. The purest gold is stunningly beautiful, expensive, and desired by people everywhere. But the process to get such gold is harsh and dangerous.

Ellen White describes the way God works to create His character in our lives. In a letter she wrote, "A harsh-spirited man is unrefined, coarse; he is not spiritual; he has not a heart of flesh, but a heart as unimpressible as a stone. His only help is to fall on the Rock, and be broken. The Lord will place all such in the crucible, and try them in fire, as gold is tried. When He can see His own image reflected in them He will remove them" (Ellen G. White, *Sons and Daughters of God* [Washington, D.C.: Review and Herald Pub. Assn., 1955], p. 100).

As I write this chapter I am sitting in front of an open fire. All that is burning is soft pinewood, yet I can feel the heat on my forehead even though I am quite a distance away. Every now and again something crackles, and bits of glowing embers leap out of the fire. How much more intense is the heat required for pure gold! Indeed, the purer the gold, the hotter the flames. Could it be that in our fanatically independent condition in which we continuously run away from our Father's ways, intense heat and pressure is the only thing that will remove what is so deeply ingrained in the inner recesses of our beings?

I think so. "I will refine them like silver and test them like gold" (Zech. 13:9). "The crucible for silver and the furnace for gold, but the Lord tests the heart" (Prov. 17:3).

So if there is one place a godly character seems to mature, it is within the fires of God's crucibles.

Character by an Easier Route?

But isn't there a less-painful way to develop character?

Helen Keller certainly didn't think so. Born June 27, 1880, in Tuscumbia, Alabama, at the age of 19 months she developed a severe fever that left her deaf and blind, and therefore mute. When Helen was 7, Anne

Sullivan arrived to be her tutor. What could she do for someone who was deaf, blind, and mute? Amazingly, with the help of her gifted teacher, Helen learned to communicate and lead an almost normal life. She could very easily have become bitter about her condition, but she knew that life consisted of more than simply living as comfortably as possible.

"Character cannot be developed in ease and quiet," she later concluded. "Only through the experience of trial and suffering can the soul be strengthened, vision cleared, ambition inspired, and success achieved" (quoted in *Leadership* 17, no. 4).

Astonishingly, the Bible even describes Jesus as maturing in the crucible. "Although he was a son, he learned obedience from what he suffered" (Heb. 5:8). I will not claim to fully understand what this means, but it appears that suffering is linked inextricably to spiritual growth.

God is looking for people with character, but not just of any sort. He seeks people who desire to be "transformed into his likeness" (2 Cor. 3:18). And it may just be that if we long to reveal such a purity of character, we may have to go through the fire.

If so, if we are to hang on when the temperatures rise, then we need to know why God longs to refine our character. Let me survey five important reasons that reflecting the character of Jesus is of critical importance for Christians today.

Why Reflecting the Character of Jesus Really Matters

1. Reflecting the character of Jesus is important because it is the focus of God's eternal plans for us.

As we noted a little earlier, the plan of salvation is not a scheme that merely focuses on how to get out of our sinful situation and into a happier place. God's intention from the very beginning was to restore His character in us. Paul sets out this purpose clearly in his letter to the Romans: "For those God foreknew he also predestined to be conformed to the likeness of his Son" (Rom. 8:29).

As a servant of God, the apostle shared the Lord's burning desire to see the divine image restored in those he served. As he rather colorfully told the Galatians: "My dear children, for whom I am again in the pains of childbirth until Christ is formed in you" (Gal. 4:19).

This process of reflecting the glory of God is both important and continuous, as Paul noticed: "And we, who with unveiled faces all reflect the Lord's glory, are being transformed into his likeness with *ever-increasing glory*, which comes from the Lord, who is the Spirit" (2 Cor. 3:18).

Yet, incredibly, the development of the character of Jesus will not stop when Jesus returns and we are transformed "in the twinkling of an eye" (1 Cor. 15:52). "Those who are under the instruction of Christ in this world will take every divine attainment with them to the heavenly mansions. And in heaven we are continually to improve. How important, then, is the development of character in this life" (Ellen G. White, *Christ's Object Lessons* [Mountain View, Calif.: Pacific Press Pub. Assn., 1900], p. 332).

2. Reflecting the character of Jesus is important because it provides the vindication of God's honor to the universe. Here is a picture that has become increasingly important to me. Imagine the scene.

It's the time just before the Second Coming. All heaven has assembled at the command of the Father, and the whole universe watches on. Jesus stands next to the Father, surrounded by a multitude of angels. Way off in the distance Satan is about to hear the words he has feared the most. The Father turns to the Son and points to a small ball swirling with bands of white and blue. On this small globe wait God's embattled people.

"Look," He says, as everyone around Him listens intently, "there is a community of people who reflect My character. Now is the time to bring them home."

In my mind I picture God sitting on the edge of His indescribable throne. He can't wait to share the news. In response to the Father's words, all heaven becomes a beehive of activity. The fulfillment of the salvation plan is literally minutes away.

From the beginning Satan has claimed that the way God behaves is unfair and unjust. Even since Satan and his angels rebelled against God and had to be expelled from heaven, the Lord has allowed plenty of time and opportunity for the devil to reveal his character. In the beginning it was not clear to many in the universe what Satan was really like. But it slowly began to show through his actions and by the people who decided to follow him. Likewise, those who chose God began to demonstrate His character.

As we noted earlier, Peter describes how under pressure faithful people will one day make a convincing argument that God is worth following. In describing the reasons for the trials that have come upon the Lord's people, he writes, "These [all kinds of trials] have come so that your faith—of greater worth than gold, which perishes even though refined by fire—may be proved genuine and may result in praise, glory and honor when Jesus Christ is revealed" (1 Peter 1:7).

When Jesus stands fully revealed, who is it that will praise, glorify, and honor Him? Is it not the universe that has followed this great struggle from the beginning? Across the face of the earth waves of people begin to rise up into the air. They have experienced the most terrible situations, but have not given up. Against the darkness of our world the universe has seen the bright pinpoints of faith gently glowing—and it is all because of what Jesus has done. The universe cannot contain itself. It will praise the Savior. Jesus has saved His people, but most important, He has rescued the universe from a future return to the battle over sin.

I believe that people who remain faithful under pressure are the most convincing evidence that God is good, and fair, and righteous. Though Job did not understand many things about his suffering, he did have one important conviction: "When he has tested me, I will come forth as gold" (Job 23:10). But I wonder whether the patriarch grasped the implications of his loyalty—that "by his patient endurance he vindicated his own character, and thus the character of Him whose representative he was" (Ellen G. White, *Sons and Daughters of God*, p. 95)?

I am increasingly convinced that honoring God is the highest purpose for my life. And that is why I think Ellen White believed that "the greatest work that can be done in our world is to glorify God by living the character of Christ" (*Testimonies,* vol. 6, p. 439).

3. Reflecting the character is important because it is the focus of the remnant. I have been trying to make the case for living out the character of Jesus within our world. Of course, doing that has always been an important witness in vindicating God's character. But let's push this idea a little further by looking specifically at those alive at the time of the end.

We see the connection between the end of time and character emphasized in Jesus' last teaching before He dies. In Matthew 25 He tells His disciples the parables about the 10 virgins, the talents, and the sheep and the goats. All three parables describe how we are to live in the time before Jesus returns. In the first one the five foolish virgins don't take extra supplies of oil with them as they wait for the bridegroom. They beg the others for extra oil, but are refused. As the five go out in search of more oil, the bridegroom arrives and closes the door. On their return they bang on the door but hear the bridegroom's stern words, "I tell you the truth, I don't know you" (Matt. 25:12).

We often interpret the oil as representing the Holy Spirit and that those without the Holy Spirit will not be taken to heaven when Jesus returns. Ellen White makes a more specific application: "In the parable, the foolish virgins are represented as begging for oil, and failing to receive it at their request. This is symbolic of those who have not prepared themselves by developing a character to stand in a time of crisis. It is as if they should go to their neighbors and say, Give me your character, or I shall be lost. Those that were wise could not impart their oil to the flickering lamps of the foolish virgins. Character is not transferable. It is not to be bought or sold; it is to be acquired. The Lord has given to every individual an opportunity to obtain a righteous character through the hours of probation; but He has not provided a way by which one human agent may impart to another the character which he has developed by going through hard experiences, by learning lessons from the great Teacher, so that he can manifest patience under trial, and exercise faith so that he can remove mountains of impossibility" (*Youth's Instructor,* Jan. 16, 1896).

The book of Daniel emphasized this urgent need for purity of character by those living at the end when a supernatural being told the prophet, "Many will be purified, made spotless and refined, but the wicked will continue to be wicked" (Dan. 12:10).

And how are God's end-time people made pure? Jesus partly gives us the answer Himself in His counsel to Laodicea: "I counsel you to buy from me gold refined in the fire" (Rev. 3:18). At the end of time God will purify His people through the crucible.

4. Reflecting the character of Jesus is important because it provides a compelling countercultural witness to the world. I watched a remarkable interview with Oxford University professor and world-renowned author Richard Dawkins. In it he argued against what he believed to be the stupidity of God and Christianity.

"The very idea of the crucifixion . . . as a redemption of the sins of mankind is a truly disgusting idea" he claimed. He continued to talk about "that dangerous thing that is common to Judaism and Christianity as well, the process of non-thinking called faith," concluding that "I can't see why faith should ever be a virtue . . ." (*Kastljos,* June 25, 2006 [www.ruv.is]).

What surprised me was that though he was a distinguished professor at a prestigious university, his answers were illogical and biased, yet he received prime-time access to share his ranting with the whole nation.

Although something within me felt very jealous for the honor of God, I began wondering how we could possibly compete for the hearts and minds of our culture. From the responses in the newspaper the next day, it seemed that many people were all too ready to support Dawkins' views.

I think the answer is that we can't, at least not on his terms. But I believe something that Marshall McLuhan once said can help. It was McLuhan who in the 1960s coined the phrase "the medium is the message," and I think Christians need to ponder a lot on this today. McLuhan appears to be saying that *how* we convey our message is just as important as, if not more vital than, *what* we say. *We* become the message. If we apply this to the spreading of the gospel, it means that *how* we share it is perhaps even more important than *what* we share. The bottom line is that if the good news of Jesus is going to be compelling, it has to be first authentic. And the gospel becomes authentic by *how* we live it, not just *what* we say.

In other words, it is our characters, or, rather, the character of Jesus *in* us, that makes the difference between a compelling or empty witness.

Perhaps that is why Ellen White wrote that "character building is the most important work ever entrusted to human beings; and never before was its diligent study so important as now. Never before was any previous generation called to meet issues so momentous; never before were young men and young women confronted by perils so great as confront them today" (*Education* [Mountain View, Calif.: Pacific Press Pub. Assn., 1903], p. 225).

She wrote this in 1903, before the two world wars, the Holocaust, Rwanda, the twin towers, the Asian tsunami, and Hurricane Katrina. If you want to share a compelling witness among such darkness, Christ's character within us will most certainly bring light.

5. Reflecting the character of Jesus is important because it is God's highest ambition for our church community. It is one thing to be a godly individual and quite another thing altogether to be godly in community. Therefore I am beginning to believe that the most compelling evidence of the truth that the Father is good and fair and righteous occurs when a group of people, who may not share anything naturally in common, and who would often get on each other's nerves, come together in a loving unity that can be attributed to nothing else but the goodness and power of God.

Paul emphasizes reflecting the character of Jesus in community in his letter to the Ephesians. He highlights the fact that reaching the fullness of Christ is what the church body does as a project together, with all the spiritual gifts being focused on this one ultimate goal. "It was he who gave some to be apostles, some to be prophets, some to be evangelists, and some to be pastors and teachers, to prepare God's people for works of service, so that the body of Christ may be built up until we all reach unity in the faith and in the knowledge of the Son of God and become mature, attaining to the whole measure of the fullness of Christ" (Eph. 4:11-13).

As Paul has just showed us, Jesus is coming to collect His body—not just an assemblage of disconnected body parts. Our community, the church, must also have Christ's character embedded deep within it. Then we will be authentic. When the rest of the world is falling apart, how else can you explain such a wide variety of people holding together in love other than by the supernatural power of God Himself?

Who knows what God can do with us then? Could such a unified community of witnesses turn the world upside down? I know it happened at Pentecost. Perhaps it's time that this glorious possibility again becomes our overwhelming reality.

An Almost-Empty Suitcase

As we look forward to the Second Coming, I believe the quest for character is both critical and urgent, for it is by our character that we are recognized. "Christ is waiting with longing desire for the manifestation of Himself in His church. When the character of Christ shall be perfectly reproduced in His people, then He will come to claim them as His own" (Ellen G. White, *Christ's Object Lessons*, p. 69).

As we continue to study this subject, I have one request. Please let's not get bogged down arguing about what she meant by "perfectly reproduced." Otherwise we risk pushing aside the centrality of character for God's people—and we can't afford to do that! Reflecting the character of Jesus is too important to be sidelined, because "a character formed according to the divine likeness is the only treasure that we can take from this world to the next" (*ibid.*, p. 332).

The priority of character is clear. When we head for our eternal home, we will have only one thing in our cosmic suitcase.

Father,
  I long to reflect Your character to the uttermost parts of my being.
  May my life be a testimony to the universe of who You are.
  Help me to have courage in this process,
  Knowing that the only thing that really counts
  Is that You are revealed and therefore glorified through me.
In Jesus' name, amen.

CHAPTER 5

How Hot Can It Get?

"Yet it was the Lord's will to crush him and cause him to suffer."
Isaiah 53:10

I was 15, and it was Monday morning. Terrible racial rioting had erupted around our home and across Colombo, the capital of Sri Lanka. In the road outside our mission compound people were having their legs broken and were set alight in burning tires. One of our neighbors saw a 70-year-old man cut to pieces with a machete. The same day, one of my friends watched people herded off rooftops and forced to jump into specially made bonfires in the streets. Another friend hid with his family in a bathroom while a mob rampaged through their house. They all escaped to the United States with just the clothes on their backs.

Over on the other side of town lived a mission pastor called Devadas, a name meaning "servant of God." He was a member of the racial minority, so he and his wife instantly became targets for attack.

The mob knew where Devadas lived, and headed there. Devadas was also out in the street and, realizing what was about to happen, ran home. Turning off the main road, he raced down an alley that opened up into a walled courtyard that joined two houses. He and his pregnant wife lived in one; the woman who owned both properties occupied the other.

As she was a member of the racial majority, she would be safe, so they begged her to hide them. Quickly she took them into her house and hid them under a bed. They just managed to squeeze under it before the mob arrived and began shouting for Devadas to come out of his house.

The owner pleaded with the crowd not to damage her property, so rather than watching them break down Devadas' door, she opened it with her key. The mob charged in, but not finding him or his wife, they began to grab things to loot.

Devadas' motorcycle, which enabled him to do his church work, was parked on the front porch. Someone was about to wheel it away when an-

49

other shouted out that he had found a brand-new sewing machine on the table and that they should take it instead, as it was easier to carry. Moments later the mob left.

Once it was safe, the owner returned, and Devadas and his wife crawled out from under the bed.

"I'm glad to say that your motorbike has been left," she began, "but unfortunately they have taken your sewing machine."

Both Devadas and his wife looked puzzled. "Sewing machine?" they asked. "We don't own a sewing machine."

"Oh yes," the woman replied in surprise. "I saw it sitting on the front table."

But no, they certainly did not own a sewing machine.

The incident has become a favorite story of mine. Every time I think about it I am filled with thankfulness for the goodness of God (though it has always made my father wonder if the angels took the sewing machine back again).

But can you imagine the reaction of Devadas and his wife? Consider how they felt being trapped at the end of the alley, then having to hide under a bed while a violent mob searched their house to kill them? How do you think they reacted when they realized that God had sent His angels to protect them? Can you guess how that incident shaped their relationship with God and their ministry to others in the years afterward?

But before those feelings of joy and thankfulness, they must have experienced great fear.

It can get hot in the crucible. Gold is a soft metal, but it still needs to be heated to around 1,947°F (1,064°C) before it will melt. If you want to separate the pure from the impure, it has got to be hot.

Of course the angels in Devadas' story could have blinded the mob and sent them past the entrance to his house. They could have arranged for him and his pregnant wife to be out of town on that Monday afternoon. But God allowed them to hear the mob walking right into their house as they both shook like leaves under a bed, just yards away.

Turning Up the Heat

For most of our questions we will have to wait to get to heaven for answers as to why God worked the way He did. But I believe one thing is clear: The Lord allows us to experience great pressure in the crucible because He is looking for people with Christlike character and willingness to serve.

A. W. Tozer certainly believed this. He once claimed that "it is doubtful whether God can bless a man greatly until He's hurt him deeply" (*Root of the Righteous,* chap. 39).

Alan Redpath really emphasizes this idea, believing that "when God wants to do an impossible task, he takes an impossible man and crushes him."

But does God use His crucibles to "crush" people?

Isaiah obviously thought so when he spoke of the coming Messiah: "Yet it was the Lord's will to crush him and cause him to suffer" (Isa. 53:10).

You may think that Jesus was a special case. But the Bible has many examples of God placing His most loved children into extremely fiery crucibles. Consider the following purposes for which God turns up the heat on His own people, thus placing them under extreme pressure.

1. To showcase the faithfulness of His people as an encouragement and example to others. When we think of extreme suffering in the Bible, our minds immediately turn to Job. If anyone suffered, he did.

But do you remember how the story began?

When Satan came to visit God, the Lord turned to him and asked an astonishing question: "Have you considered my servant Job?" (Job 1:8).

Wait a moment. God said what?

It wasn't Satan who brought the man to God's attention. As the patriarch walked around on the earth minding his own business, God looked at Satan and pointed at Job.

"Can you see Job down there?"

"Job worships You because You take good care of him," Satan quickly responded. "'But stretch out your hand and strike everything he has, and he will surely curse you to your face.' The Lord said to Satan, 'Very well, then, everything he has is in your hands, but on the man himself do not lay a finger'" (Job 1:11, 12).[*]

You can read the story in the book of Job. First, his oxen and donkeys get stolen by Sabean bandits. Next, fire destroys his sheep. Then a Chaldean raiding party rides off with his camels. Bad as this was, it was not nearly as devastating as the news that all his sons and daughters had perished during a party at their oldest brother's house.

Surely, God, this is too much to bear! Job must have thought. But more was to come.

Painful boils struck Job. And then there was his wife and a group of friends who were not exactly helpful. "His wife said to him, 'Are you still holding on to your integrity? Curse God and die!'" (Job 2:9).

But despite multiple attacks from Satan, Job did not curse the Lord. He remained faithful to the very end. As a consequence, Job has inspired and encouraged millions of God's children for thousands of years.

2. To accomplish a great transformation in a short period of time. In chapter 1 we looked at the suffering of Joseph. His early life offers an interesting example of God's using an extremely hot crucible to bring about a dramatic transformation in a very short time.

Ellen White reveals that the unwise actions of his father had created significant character defects that needed correction. God was able to transform those personal defects through the harsh crucible of being thrown into the pit by his brothers, and of being callously sold to passing traders.

The time period for Joseph's transformation was quick. "He had learned in a few hours that which years might not otherwise have taught him. . . . One day's experience had been the turning point in Joseph's life. Its terrible calamity had transformed him from a petted child to a man, thoughtful, courageous, and self-possessed" (*Patriarchs and Prophets,* pp. 213, 214).

A brief, but intense, period in the crucible provided an essential stepping-stone in Joseph's journey to becoming ruler in Egypt and a savior to his people.

3. To memorably impress us with truths to teach others afterward.

"Some time later God tested Abraham. He said to him, 'Abraham!'

"'Here I am,' he replied.

"Then God said, 'Take your son, your only son, Isaac, whom you love, and go to the region of Moriah. Sacrifice him there as a burnt offering on one of the mountains I will tell you about'" (Gen. 22:1, 2).

Let's examine this conversation.

Did God really tell Abraham to kill his son? Yes, He did.

Did God intend for Abraham to kill his son? Well, actually, no.

Did Abraham know that God didn't mean it? Not at all.

And that was the point.

The Lord was bringing the crucible to boiling point. In order for Abraham to fully experience the anguish of giving up his only son, the incident came at a very specific time, calculated to exert maximum impact, for "God had reserved His last, most trying test for Abraham until the burden of years was heavy on him, and he longed for rest" (*ibid.,* p. 147).

So what was God looking for? "In his doubt and anguish he [Abraham] bowed down to the earth, and prayed, . . . for some confirmation of the command. . . . He remembered the angels sent to him . . . , and he went to the place . . . , hoping to meet them again, and receive some further direction; but none came to his relief. . . . The agony which he endured during the dark days of that fearful trial was permitted that he might understand from his own experience something of the greatness of the sacrifice made by the infinite God for man's redemption" (*ibid.*, pp. 148-154).

Even Jesus remarked about this experience to His disciples. "Your father Abraham rejoiced at the thought of seeing my day; he saw it and was glad" (John 8:56). Abraham "saw" the sacrifice of Jesus by experiencing a similar event. But it was only by God piling on the pressure that Abraham's faith could echo so loudly and clearly through history as he passed on to his family the significance of the great sacrifice that God was offering them.

4. To remind us of our complete dependence upon Him.

Paul clearly identifies the purpose of his sufferings to the Corinthians. "We were under great pressure, far beyond our ability to endure, so that we despaired even of life. Indeed, in our hearts we felt the sentence of death. But this happened that we might not rely on ourselves but on God, who raises the dead" (2 Cor. 1:8, 9).

A few chapters later he then gives a long list of what had happened to him: "Five times I received from the Jews the forty lashes minus one. Three times I was beaten with rods, once I was stoned, three times I was shipwrecked, I spent a night and a day in the open sea, I have been constantly on the move. I have been in danger from rivers, in danger from bandits, in danger from my own countrymen, in danger from Gentiles; in danger in the city, in danger in the country, in danger at sea; and in danger from false brothers. I have labored and toiled and have often gone without sleep; I have known hunger and thirst and have often gone without food; I have been cold and naked. Besides everything else, I face daily the pressure of my concern for all the churches. Who is weak, and I do not feel weak? Who is led into sin, and I do not inwardly burn?" (2 Cor. 11:24-29).

Paul clearly recognized a divine purpose behind the overwhelming circumstances that threatened him and his companions. He saw the pressures as a call to complete dependence on God, and that dependence gave his ministry power. As he declared to the Corinthians: "When I came to you, brothers, I did not come with eloquence or superior wisdom as I proclaimed to you the testimony about God. For I resolved to know nothing while I was with you except Jesus Christ and him crucified. I came to you in weakness and fear, and with much trembling. My message and my preaching were not with wise and persuasive words, but with a demonstration of the Spirit's power, so that your faith might not rest on men's wisdom, but on God's power" (1 Cor. 2:1-5).

5. To persuade us to surrender our sin.

We have already noted in chapter 3 that God uses crucibles to purify us from sin. The problem is that we cling to some of our sins extremely tightly. In this next example (from the book of Hosea) God explains that He is also willing to heat up the crucible to remove even those sins from our lives.

In Hosea 1-3 He employs the image of a husband and wife to describe His relationship with His people. God's challenge is that the wife is not interested in remaining faithful to her husband. "She said, 'I will go after my lovers, who give me my food and my water, my wool and my linen, my oil and my drink'" (Hosea 2:5).

However, God—who stands in the place of the husband—wants His people back, and will do anything to persuade them. "Therefore I will block her path with thornbushes; I will wall her in so that she cannot find her way. She will chase after her lovers but not catch them; she will look for them but not find them. Then she will say, 'I will go back to my husband as at first, for then I was better off than now'" (verses 6, 7).

If God sees us heading in the wrong direction, it seems that He is willing to block our way with extremely painful barriers—painful, that is, if we run into them in a hurry. Yet in the story the faithless wife is still not interested in returning to God. "She has not acknowledged that I was the one who gave her the grain, the new wine and oil, who lavished on her the silver and gold—which they used for Baal" (verse 8).

So God ups the pressure again. "Therefore I will take away my grain when it ripens, and my new wine when it is ready. I will take back my wool and my linen, intended to cover her nakedness. So now I will expose her lewdness before the eyes of her lovers; no one will take her out of my hands" (verses 9, 10).

In order to bring the woman back to her senses and her true husband, God subjects her to considerable loss, taking away her comforts and necessities, including her clothes, which leaves her naked. Embarrassing is an understatement. Indeed, this husband risks being seriously misunderstood, for what loving man would allow his wife naked in public?

I suppose it depends how desperately he wants her back. Love, even divine love, will risk everything for what is truly important.

Struggling With a God Who Seems to Change

Yet because of our pain we may not always understand God's great love for us.

During a Youth Week of Prayer I asked some teens to draw pictures of God without portraying Him as a person. To my surprise, every one of them included a heart somewhere on the page. Their united conviction was clear: God is love. But as we grow older and life is not as simple or as comfortable as it used to be, our sense of Him as a deity of love may often seem to blur, if not fade completely.

Joy, the wife of C. S. Lewis, was dying. Because of the pain Lewis experienced as he watched, he found himself tempted to redefine who God was. "Not that I am (I think) in much danger of ceasing to believe in God. The real danger is coming to believe such dreadful things about Him. The conclusion I dread is not 'So there's no God after all,' but 'So this is what God's really like'" (*A Grief Observed,* chap. 1).

Many of us, because of our pain, experience this same temptation to redefine God. We may totally miss that He is at work for us. Or like Lewis, we may tend to think that He is misguided. So at the times when we are hurting, how do we prevent ourselves from falling into this trap of believing all sorts of "dreadful things" about God because of the intense heat of the crucible?

How to Avoid Redefining God in the Crucible

If we review the Bible stories just covered, you will notice different ways in which the people responded to the intense pressure without giving in to the temptation to think that God had lost His love and compassion.

1. When the crucible was very hot, Job didn't stop worshipping. One of the first things that many people do when they experience pain is to stop attending church. Why bother when God appears uninterested in removing our pain? But Job worships anyway.

The patriarch maintained his belief in the goodness of God by determining to worship God in spite of his circumstances. "At this, Job got up and tore his robe and shaved his head. Then he fell to the ground in worship and said: 'Naked I came from my mother's womb, and naked I will depart. The Lord gave and the Lord has taken away; may the name of the Lord be praised'" (Job 1:20, 21).

Whatever the pressures, Job knew that his help and strength would be found on his knees before his Father.

2. When the crucible was very hot, Joseph kept looking up. When Joseph could have crumpled under the pressure, his thoughts went upward. He didn't buckle, because "his soul thrilled with the high resolve to prove himself true to God—under all circumstances to act as became a subject of the King of heaven. He would serve the Lord with undivided heart; he would meet the trials of his lot with fortitude and perform every duty with fidelity" (Ellen G. White, *Patriarchs and Prophets,* p. 214).

Joseph was practicing what Paul encouraged the Colossians to do also: "Set your hearts on things above, where Christ is seated at the right hand of God. Set your minds on things above, not on earthly things" (Col. 3:1, 2). And because of Joseph's resolve, God used him to save the land of Egypt from famine. Thus his own family, the family that grew into the nation of Israel in later years, remained alive.

3. When the crucible was very hot, Abraham didn't stop obeying. Abraham did not lose his nerve, because he personally knew the voice of God and was not tempted to believe that it was the devil or his imagination. So when God spoke, Abraham's reply was "Here I am" (Gen. 22:1).

And so God promised him, "Because you have done this and have not withheld your son, your only son, I will surely bless you and make your descendants as numerous as the stars in the sky and as the sand on the seashore. Your descendants will take possession of the cities of their enemies, and through your offspring all nations on earth will be blessed, because you have obeyed me" (verses 16-18).

4. When the crucible was very hot, Paul didn't forget that God was still sovereign. The apostle kept on going under great personal suffering through the years because he was convinced "that in all things God works for the good of those who love him, who have been called according to his purpose" (Rom. 8:28). In even the darkest moments Paul knew that God was at work.

So by the end of his ministry, facing certain martyrdom, he was able to write to Timothy, "For I am already being poured out like a drink offering, and the time has come for my departure. I have fought the good fight, I have finished the race, I have kept the faith. Now there is in store for me the crown of righteousness, which the Lord, the righteous Judge, will award to me on that day—and not only to me, but also to all who have longed for his appearing" (2 Tim. 4:6-8).

5. When the crucible was very hot, the people—failed to repent. Unlike the previous four examples, we end on a down note. Alas, when the heat of the crucible increased for Israel, God's "wife" often failed to do what it desperately needed to do—repent.

The cry of God's heart was always for His people to return to Him. He did not want them to remain walled in by the painful circumstances that He was permitting. Imagine Hosea's hurt as he wrote, "Will they not return to Egypt and will not Assyria rule over them because they refuse to repent?" (Hosea 11:5).

God repeats this call in Ezekiel: "Therefore, O house of Israel, I will judge you, each one according to his ways, declares the Sovereign Lord. Repent! Turn away from all your offenses; then sin will not be your downfall. Rid yourselves of all the offenses you have committed, and get a new heart and a new spirit. Why will you die, O house of Israel? For I take no pleasure in the death of anyone, declares the Sovereign Lord. Repent and live!" (Eze. 18:30-32).

So when the heat rises in the crucible, it might well be the time for God's people to examine their loyalty to God.

Our Father Is Not a Bully

After what we have considered, it may be tempting to view God as a bully, someone who doesn't care about how we feel as long as He gets His own way with us. But such a conclusion would be a gross misrepresentation of His intentions. We are the most precious possessions He has. He will risk everything, though He may appear harsh and unkind in the process, if one day we will sit up and listen, and finally want to return home. The intense heat in His crucibles is a sign, not of His intense displeasure toward us, but of His intense displeasure at the sin that warps our ability to reflect His goodness, holiness, and love. So His crucibles may often need to be hot.

"God has always tried his people in the furnace of affliction. It is in the heat of the furnace that the dross is separated from the true gold of the Christian character. Jesus watches the test, He knows what is needed to purify the precious metal, that it may reflect the radiance of His love. It is by close, testing trials that God disciplines His servants. He sees that some have powers which may be used in the advancement of His work, and He puts these persons upon trial, in His providence He brings them into positions that test their character. . . . He shows them their own weakness, and teaches them to lean upon Him. . . . Thus his object is attained. They are educated, trained, and disciplined, prepared to fulfill the grand purpose for which their powers were given them" (Ellen G. White, *Patriarchs and Prophets,* pp. 129, 130).

I want to conclude with a text from Isaiah that has always been of great encouragement. It expresses the great paternal love of God for us, but in spite of His love, we may still find ourselves called to "pass through the waters" and "walk through the fire." But the passage urges us not to worry. He is still with us.

"But now, this is what the Lord says—he who created you, O Jacob, he who formed you, O Israel: 'Fear not, for I have redeemed you; I have summoned you by name; you are mine. When you pass through the waters, I will be with you; and when you pass through the rivers, they will not sweep over you. When you walk through the fire, you will not be burned; the flames will not set you ablaze. For I am the Lord, your God, the Holy One of Israel, your Savior; I give Egypt for your ransom, Cush and Seba in your stead. Since you are precious and honored in my sight, and because I love you, I will give men in exchange for you, and people in exchange for your life. Do not be afraid, for I am with you; I will bring your children from the east and gather you from the west. I will say to the north, 'Give them up!' and to the south, 'Do not hold them back.' Bring my sons from afar and my daughters from the ends of the earth—everyone who is called by my name, whom I created for my glory, whom I formed and made" (Isa. 43:1-7).

> Father,
> Would You really act as we have been discussing, so I can be more like You?
> Would You really do anything to bring me home?
> Open my eyes, so that I may see Your love at all times,
> Strengthen my faith, that I may trust You, even when it seems impossible.
> In Jesus' name, amen.

---

* It is interesting to note that while Satan could not take Job's life, it appears that he was allowed to destroy his family.

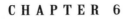

CHAPTER 6

Disciplines for Staying on the Path

"To this end I labor, struggling with all his energy,
which so powerfully works in me."
Colossians 1:29

We have reached a pivot point in the book. Behind us we have considered the reasons for suffering in our lives, focusing particularly on the suffering that God allows and directs for the maturing of His character within us. In the chapters ahead we will consider some of the specific characteristics of God, graces of the Holy Spirit, that He longs to see us reflect. But before we move into this next section, we are going to consider four spiritual disciplines—habits that create an environment for spiritual change, that are critical for the development of these graces. Such disciplines prepare us to survive the crucibles that we meet along the path to the Shepherd's house.

Introducing the Disciplines

Let me make it clear from the start that these spiritual disciplines do not change us by themselves. Only the Holy Spirit can transform us. But what they do is make us open and available for God to develop His graces within.

Richard Foster also describes the reflection of God's graces as a journey along a path. On one side of this path we can fall into the chasm of human efforts. Or on the other side we can tumble into the chasm caused by a failure to do anything for ourselves. "As we travel this path," Foster observes, "the blessing of God will come upon us and reconstruct us into the image of Jesus. We must remember that the path does not produce the change; it only places us where the change can occur. This is the path of disciplined grace" (*Celebration of Discipline* [New York: HarperCollins Publishers, Inc., 1998], p. 8).

Staying on the path of "disciplined grace" requires constant choices. At the heart of the spiritual disciplines, it seems to me that it is our decisions that keep us clear of self-pity, or the desire to quit, when our crucible heats up.

I noticed the striking and contrasting consequences of our decisions during an afternoon talk show. A man and woman sat next to each other on the sofa sharing their stories. Both had experienced the murder of a child, and they each described how they had been coping. The woman's son had been killed 20 years before, and as she said herself, her anger and bitterness was far greater now than when the murder had occurred—and she had been on sleeping pills ever since. By the hardness of the look on her face, she certainly seemed to be telling the truth.

The man was a picture of the complete opposite. His daughter had died from an IRA bomb a few years before. Rather than responding with bitterness and anger, he spoke about forgiveness toward her murderers, and how God had transformed his hurt. I don't want to underestimate how difficult it must have been for him to endure such suffering, but somehow he had become an illustration of how God can bring healing to the darkest moments of our lives.

Revealing Purest Gold

Job declared, "When he has tested me, I will come forth as gold" (Job 23:10). Revealing such purest gold motivated him, and it shaped the choices he made in the crucible every day. After the news of his great financial losses, after he heard of his children's deaths, after his wife tried to persuade him to "curse God and die," after months with no relief for his physical pain, he kept choosing to trust his Father.

So as we journey along this path of "disciplined grace," what are the spiritual disciplines that will help us to survive the crucibles, keeping us in a position to grow continually into the gold of a Christlike character?

1. Gold is refined through the discipline of an active will. When I was small, we children used to tell each other a riddle: What's the only thing that God cannot make? The answer we proudly revealed was "two mountains without a valley between."

But there are some other things that God can't do. He cannot force our wills. He cannot compel us either to repent or to obey—otherwise we would simply become pawns in a game of celestial chess. In the crucible our personal choice to repent and obey is key to spiritual change. Because of this, our wills have become the battleground on which the supernatural forces around us collide, for "this will, that forms so important a factor in the character of man, was at the Fall given into the control of Satan; and he has ever since been working in man to will and to do of his own pleasure, but to the utter ruin and misery of man" (Ellen

G. White, *Mind, Character, and Personality* [Nashville: Southern Pub. Assn., 1977], vol. 2, p. 685).

In spite of this, however, it is all too easy for our wills to become sleepy.

This came to mind as I was watching a famous televangelist on early-morning TV. Standing behind his transparent pulpit, he was speaking in tender tones with tears running down his cheeks. The camera panned across the huge indoor arena in which row after row of people sat there waiting expectantly. Their hands were slightly lifted up, palms held open, their heads were tilted back, and tears ran down their cheeks. For them, it was obviously a very emotional experience. As I stared at the TV, the thought sprang to mind, *What are they waiting for?*

If I had asked them, I think they would have replied that they expected to be transformed by a new filling of the Holy Spirit that the preacher would eventually distribute by a wave of his hand.

It struck me that I was watching a very subtle but dangerous idea that pervades much of modern Christianity. Too often we just seem to be waiting around for the Holy Spirit to do something to us to make us become godly. We can even misuse prayer in this regard. If we have a problem that we find ourselves struggling with, others encourage us to pray more.

Now, I don't want to sound confusing. I have started prayer networks and written articles on the need for prayer throughout my ministry. But that is not all we need to do. If we just sit around praying, we may actually be insinuating that God hasn't given us enough of the Spirit yet, and that we need to keep praying until we can persuade Him to send us enough power to fix the problem. The danger is that we may be sentimentalizing prayer, waiting for the Holy Spirit to do something that God actually wants us to do now.

So while the Holy Spirit is at the crux of spiritual transformation, it is our response to Him that determines the depth of change.

To help us understand this, consider how Jesus describes the coming of the Holy Spirit to His disciples in John 16. Jesus depicts Him as the Counselor and the Spirit of truth. "But I tell you the truth: It is for your good that I am going away. Unless I go away, the Counselor will not come to you; but if I go, I will send him to you. When he comes, he will convict the world of guilt in regard to sin and righteousness and judgment.... But when he, the Spirit of truth, comes, he will guide you into all truth. He will not speak on his own; he will speak only what he hears, and he will tell you what is yet to come" (John 16:7-13).

When Jesus explained the role of the Holy Spirit, He told the disciples that the primary function of the Counselor is to convict us of sin. However, the Spirit cannot make us repent. And as the Spirit of truth, the Spirit will reveal the great truths about God—but He cannot make us believe them. In both cases, unless we make conscious choices to repent and believe, the great power of the resurrected Jesus can do little for us. Our will stands as a door between the revelation of what we need to do and the transformation that follows.

2. Gold is refined through the discipline of struggle. I had a friend who was putting all of her energy into reflecting the character of Christ. The changes in her were amazing, but after a while she declared, "I'm not going to try much anymore—it's too tiring!"

In a world that greatly desires comfort, the idea of sweating and straining for the gospel can seem far from our concept of how transformation should occur. Yet Paul regularly refers to his determined efforts for God.

To the Colossians he writes, "To this end I labor, struggling with all his energy, which so powerfully works in me" (Col. 1:29). The word Paul uses for "struggle" is the source of the English word "agonize," and was a word used to describe the effort of athletes in their competitions. While it is really important to notice that Paul does not struggle alone, but employs God's power, the apostle still expends great effort. This means that the power of God is not necessarily a nice warm feeling that makes us tingle inside. It may have no feeling at all, but is still present and strengthening us, even in the middle of our suffering.

In our Christian experience we struggle against three significant powers.

First, we struggle in overcoming our emotions. Whether we like it or not, emotional stimuli swamp our lives. TV, music, advertising are all designed to evoke an emotional response aimed at getting us to act without thinking. How many times have we said, "What do I feel like eating tonight? What do I feel like buying today? What do I feel like doing now?" And what we end up eating, buying, or doing may have little in common with God's purposes for us. So when I am struggling to do the right thing while circumstances play havoc with my emotions, I still have to choose to do right no matter how I feel.

Second, we struggle in overcoming deeply engrained habits. Being saturated in a culture that continually tries to seduce us with the need to feel good all the time, and tempted to think that God should do all the hard work, I read quotations such as the following with great suspicion. "In order to receive God's help, man must realize his weakness and deficiency; he must apply his own mind to the great change to be wrought in himself; he must be aroused to earnest and persevering prayer and effort. Wrong habits and customs must be shaken off; and it is only by determined endeavor to correct these errors and to conform to right principles that the victory can be gained. Many never attain to the position that they might occupy, because they wait for God to do for them that which He has given them power to do for themselves. All who are fitted for usefulness must be trained by the severest mental and moral discipline, and God will assist them by uniting divine power with human effort" (Ellen G. White, *Patriarchs and Prophets,* p. 248).

Yet Jesus personally challenges us all with such decisive action. "If your right eye causes you to sin, gouge it out and throw it away" (Matt. 5:29). Yes, we probably all want to agree with Him and live a life of radical discipleship. But practicing it can be challenging. Indeed, as long as we live inside a sinful body, we can expect it to be.

Third, we struggle in overcoming evil supernatural powers. While we combat our emotions and bad habits, our greatest conflict is against Satan. Very early in my ministry God opened my eyes to the reality that "our struggle is not against flesh and blood, but against the rulers, against the authorities, against the powers of this dark world and against the spiritual forces of evil in the heavenly realms" (Eph. 6:12).

Many times I have awakened gasping for air as a supernatural power seemed to be putting its hands around my throat. It stopped only when I called out to Jesus for help.

On a number of occasions even talking about the battle against the supernatural has caused things to start moving in the room. One time after hearing this supernatural battle described at a youth camp, four girls ran back to the assembly hall looking scared. As they had made their way to their cabin, a big ball of light had started to circle them in the trees.

I want to make it clear that not everything that goes wrong is because of Satan's interference. Indeed, sometimes to focus on his work can be very unhelpful, even dangerous, as people concentrate on him rather than on God. I think that that is why the Bible itself does not often speak directly about Satan and his work. However, at the same time, I have also found that many people are so ignorant of Satan's involvement in our lives that we can easily develop a blasé attitude and underestimate our enemy, at great personal cost.

It's also important to recognize that often Satan works through other people to cause us hurt. I became aware of this once when a woman phoned me and unexpectedly announced, "Well, you probably don't like us, and we don't like you!"

As she was a manic depressive, I knew she was not well. I was as polite as possible and put her comment out of my mind. Or at least I thought I had. The problem was that as the day rolled on, her comment bothered me more and more. By 5:00 p.m. I felt completely terrible. It was so unusual for me that I actually began to wonder if Satan was at work. Although I was supposed to lead a prayer meeting that evening, I now experienced such overwhelming feelings of despair and heaviness that it had paralyzed me to the point that I was on the verge of canceling the appointment. As I drove along wondering what to do, I found myself blurting out loud, "In the name of Jesus, get behind me, Satan."

To this day I have no idea why I said this, but the effect was immediate and dramatic. It was as though an incredible physical weight lifted right off me, and an incredible joy instantly filled me. It was so powerful that when I arrived at the house for the prayer meeting, people looked at the extraordinary smile on my face that I was trying to hide, and asked in astonishment, "What happened to you?"

Satan was definitely at work, but if God had not led me to think about the possibility that the devil was involved, working through the person to say those hurtful words, and then stirring them around in my mind during the day, I would have begun to feel quite resentful toward that woman and would have missed the prayer meeting.

When we are under pressure, Satan will try to remain invisible. He hopes we will become embroiled in battling people rather than recognizing the sinister power at work behind the situation. However, unless we understand what is really happening, we will be tempted to fight back against people, and the process of refining gold in our lives will grind to a halt.

I am not suggesting that we should consider struggling enjoyable. Nor should we search for opportunities to do it, for that would be like whipping ourselves in some bizarre penance ritual. However, struggle is an inevitable part of living as a sinful human being in a sinful world. But if we choose to remain faithful no matter how hard it gets, our Father will use those situations to foster His character within us.

Ellen White observes how God employs our struggles to strengthen us and encourages those who face such situations. "Often men pray and weep because of the perplexities and obstacles that confront them. But it is God's purpose for them to meet perplexities and obstacles, and if they will hold the beginning of their confidence steadfast unto the end, determined to carry forward the work of the Lord, He will make their way clear. Success will come to them as they perseveringly struggle against apparently insurmountable difficulties; and with success will come the greatest joy" (*The Upward Look* [Washington, D.C.: Review and Herald Pub. Assn., 1982], p. 116).

3. Gold is refined through the discipline of perseverance. Many of our crucibles demand that we discipline ourselves to persevere. An incident one dark night by the Jabbok River powerfully illustrates this.

Jacob was having problems with Laban and his family, and the situation was getting awkward. "Then the Lord said to Jacob, 'Go back to the land of your fathers and to your relatives, and I will be with you'" (Gen. 31:3). The problem was that the patriarch had not seen his brother, Esau, ever since he had fled from him with a stolen birthright. Obeying God's command, Jacob started home with his huge entourage. As he made the historic journey, even angels came to meet him (Gen. 32:1). Sending a message on ahead to his brother, he soon received a reply—his brother was coming with 400 men.

After working out a plan in case of attack, Jacob took his two wives and 11 sons across the river Jabbok. Then he spent the night alone. But an unexpected encounter led to a desperate battle. "When the man saw that he could not overpower him, he touched the socket of Jacob's hip so that his hip was wrenched as he wrestled with the man. Then the man said, 'Let me go, for it is daybreak.' But Jacob replied, 'I will not let you go unless you bless me.' The man asked him, 'What is your name?' 'Jacob,' he answered. Then the man said, 'Your name will no longer be Jacob, but Israel, because you have struggled with God and with men and have overcome.' Jacob said, 'Please tell me your name.' But he replied, 'Why do you ask my name?' Then he blessed him there. So Jacob called the place Peniel, saying, 'It is because I saw God face to face, and yet my life was spared'" (verses 25-30).

What is so interesting in this story is that once God had touched Jacob's hip and it dislocated, the patriarch could not have done much wrestling. I think it was now more a question of hanging on to his opponent than anything else.

Jacob's story highlights the tension that you may have been sensing throughout this chapter. On the one hand, all spiritual transformation is a divine work. But it rarely takes place without hard choices and much effort on our part. Jacob hung on to God until he received His blessing. And the Lord rewarded his persistence. Indeed, it seems that God was testing Jacob to see if the patriarch's faith in His promises would persevere despite the man's pain. Had Jacob let go after the injury of his hip, he would never have received the blessing. It was after having survived the night, and then enduring excruciating agony, that Jacob received the blessing promised so many years before.

Did God deliberately place Jacob in this exhausting situation? I suppose we will have to wait until we reach heaven for a certain answer, but consider this observation: "The Lord frequently places us in difficult positions to stimulate us to greater exertion. In His providence special annoyances sometimes occur to test our patience and faith. God gives us lessons of trust. He would teach us where to look for help and strength in time of need. Thus we obtain practical knowledge of His divine will, which we so much need in our life experience. Faith grows strong in earnest conflict with doubt and fear" (Ellen G. White, *Testimonies,* vol. 4, pp. 116, 117).

For me the reality of this conflict with doubt and fear emerged while talking to a fellow pastor. His marriage of just a few years was almost finished, and he was totally exhausted in his search for a solution. He explained his situation and the constant battles he was having with God and the desperation that filled his prayers. You could see just by looking at him that he was worn out. But the more he talked, the more convinced I became that he was struggling because of a lack of faith. He was pleading to God for help, but I wasn't sure that he really believed that the Lord would do anything for him. I tried to explain to him the need to exert faith in such situations, and that just asking God for help was not the only thing that mattered. After urging him to claim God's promises with certainty, we had a short prayer together and parted.

Three weeks later I met him again, and he was radiant. Excitedly he explained to me how he had gotten down on his knees and pleaded earnestly for faith—faith for himself and for his wife—and how he was now learning to exert the faith he already had. Within just a few days their marriage had undergone a total transformation. Even today my mind can see his glowing face. God had performed a miracle, but it required him to persevere and hang on tightly.

4. Gold is refined through the discipline of communion. I have deliberately spent this chapter emphasising our need to keep choosing as a key part of the gold refining process. To me, at least, our emotional, feel-good culture seems to be undermining our discipleship to Christ at every turn and firm choices are critical if we are not to let our feelings control us.

Ultimately, however, the discipline of an active will, the discipline of determined effort, and the discipline of perseverance are all for one purpose—to keep our eyes fixed constantly on Christ. This is a discipline in itself, because we always have plenty of reasons to avoid such intimate communion with God.

During a particular period of ministry I found myself completely overwhelmed by a lot of gossip that I had heard about myself. Having a tendency to chew on such things, I became so depressed that I even decided to talk to my doctor. It also resulted in my communion with God evaporating.

Eventually I realized that I could not continue to neglect God. I decided to renew my Bible study time. I also wanted to learn the secret to Moses' success in leading people who gossiped and opposed him continually.

The first morning I opened my Bible and started to pray. Before I had said much at all, a voice interrupted my thoughts.

The trials of the past few years have not come because the people have been critical or nasty. They have come because you have not spent time face to face with Me.

As the enormity of it all began to sink in, it left me stunned. But God had more to say.

I have allowed you to watch everything fall apart around you so that you will know how strong you really are.

I felt crushed. How could I have forgotten everything that He had taught me about dependence upon Him in my early ministry? To say that it was a humbling experience would be a gross understatement. But God was right. I had failed to remain intimate with Him, and I was now suffering as a result.

I had forgotten that it is only "by beholding we become changed. Through close study and earnest contemplation of the character of Christ, His image is reflected in our own lives, and a higher tone is imparted to the spirituality of the church. If the truth of God has not transformed our characters into the likeness of Christ, all our professed knowledge of Him and the truth is but as sounding brass and a tinkling cymbal" (Ellen G. White, in *Review and Herald,* Apr. 24, 1913). No matter whether we are a new Christian or a seasoned Christian leader, this reality is true for us all.

Keep Looking Up

If we want to live out the values of God's kingdom today, we have to be spiritually tough. This was emphasized when the British Broadcasting Corporation reported on a poll of music videos that "broke the rules" (July 24, 2006). The videos were considered rule breakers because of their blasphemy against God and sexual impurity. Rather than shunning such topics, the BBC reported that all top 100 of the rule-breaking videos would be played in celebration of MTV's 25-year anniversary. Within such a culture, staying on the path will certainly not happen by accident.

To choose, and to keep choosing, for God when we find ourselves within the pressures of the crucible calls for rigorous Christian living—for a determined commitment to see nothing but Christ. So for those of us who are tempted to stop looking up because of the pressures around us, Paul has an encouraging reminder: "Since, then, you have been raised with Christ, set your hearts on things above, where Christ is seated at the right hand of God. Set your minds on things above, not on earthly things. For you died, and your life is now hidden with Christ in God. When Christ, who is your life, appears, then you also will appear with him in glory" (Col. 3:1-4).

Father,
   Living in the crucible is hard.
   But may I never forget Your presence with me.
   May I never hesitate to fall at Your feet
   With a willingness to repent, to learn, and to obey.
   Grant me the strength of a disciplined mind that can stand against the pressure of my culture,
   The bravery to do the right thing, and the tenacity to hold on, so that Your work will be accomplished in my life through the path of disciplined grace.
In Jesus' name, amen.

CHAPTER 7

Hope—in God Himself

*"Paul, an apostle of Christ Jesus by the command of
God our Savior and of Christ Jesus our hope."*
1 Timothy 1:1

Introduction to the Graces

In the previous chapters we have explored how God uses crucibles for the holy purpose of refining His character within us. Such crucibles may come because God sees something specific within us that He wishes to attend to. However, such crucibles may also emerge as a direct result of our own prayers for spiritual growth. "Often when we pray for the graces of the Spirit, God works to answer our prayers by placing us in circumstances to develop these fruits; but we do not understand His purpose, and wonder, and are dismayed" (Ellen G. White, *Christ's Object Lessons*, p. 61). Notice that God does not refine us simply by sending us a special filling of his Holy Spirit. Rather, He uses the Holy Spirit in conjunction with specific life situations—situations that we might not like!

Ellen White continues expanding on this idea. "The Lord disciplines His workers, that they may be prepared to fill the places appointed them. He desires to fit them to do more acceptable service. There are those who wish to be a ruling power, and who need the sanctification of submission. God brings about a change in their lives. Perhaps He places before them duties that they would not choose. If they are willing to be guided by Him, He will give them grace and strength to perform these duties in a spirit of submission and helpfulness. Thus they are being qualified to fill places where their disciplined abilities will make them of great service.

"Some God trains by bringing to them disappointment and apparent failure. It is His purpose that they shall learn to master difficulties. He inspires them with a determination to prove every apparent failure a success. . . .

"A life of monotony is not the most conducive to spiritual growth. Some can reach the highest standard of spirituality only through a change in the regular order of things. When in His providence God sees that changes are essential for the success of the character-building, He disturbs the smooth current of the life. He sees that a worker needs to be more closely associated with Him; and to bring this about, He separates him from friends and acquaintances" (Ellen G. White, *Gospel Workers* [Washington, D.C.: Review and Herald Pub. Assn., 1915], pp. 269, 270).

The unpleasant situations we face can therefore be the direct answer to our prayers for spiritual growth. The prayer for one grace of the Spirit may require one situation and the prayer for a different grace, another.

In the remaining chapters we will look at six different graces that God desires to refine in us, each of which may call for a different type of crucible. In this chapter we will begin exploring hope.

Hope

Orange, the European mobile phone operator, has a catchy tagline for their company: "The future's bright: the future's Orange." Their marketing campaign has logged on to the desire of every human heart for a bright and positive future. Orange is trying to sell telephones with hope, seeking to persuade would-be purchasers that should they own one of Orange's phones they would then immediately begin to live hope-filled lives. But where does the Christian find hope?

People often believe that they can find a bright future through a large savings account, a promising career, or a good reputation. As Christians we may claim that pursuing such things is foolish, though many of us still do it anyway. However, one of the red herrings that even serious Christians follow in their search for a bright future is based on knowing God's will. "If only I knew God's will for my life," we say, "I could have peace."

To those of us who are trying to find security through knowing God's will for our lives, Oswald Chambers has a disturbing truth. "Have you been asking God what He is going to do? He will never tell you. God does not tell you what He is going to do; He reveals to you who He is" (*My Utmost for His Highest,* reading for Jan. 2).

I think Chambers is right. Of course, we want to live God's will for our lives, but finding and living the divine will is not like locating a lost wallet that we then thankfully replace in our pocket. Hope is not because we have found "something," but because we have confidence in "someone"—God Himself. So in this chapter we are going to explore four reasons for hope, each one involving a facet of who our Father is—for God Himself is our hope.

Hope Is a Person

1. I face a future of hope because my Father is sovereign. "I heard and my heart pounded, my lips quivered at the sound; decay crept into my bones, and my legs trembled. Yet I will wait patiently for the day of calamity to come on the nation invading us" (Hab. 3:16).

An African proverb declares, "When two elephants fight, it is the grass that gets trampled on." In the crucible we may certainly feel as if we are being trampled on, but we must not forget to see the bigger picture of the struggle between the elephants.

Early in my ministry I went to an interdenominational pastors' meeting. They were teaching how important it is for postmodern people to understand the Bible as a single and complete narrative. The teacher highlighted what he believed to be five essential parts on which all other stories in the Bible hang. These were (a) Creation, (b) the fall of humanity, (c) the life, death, and resurrection of Jesus, (d) judgment, and (e) the Second Coming.

However, I would like to add another two essential elements that act like the front and back covers of a book: the fall of Satan in heaven at the very beginning of the story, and the destruction of him and his angels in the lake of fire at the very end. This ensures that I will always remember both the supernatural nature of the story and how the problem of pain is going to end. Most important, it reminds me that God is sovereign over all these things.

A sense of the sovereignty of God is what kept Habakkuk going even when under pressure. I really like the prophet because he articulates what is on my mind as well. In the first couple chapters of his book Habakkuk explodes to God about the terrible things happening around him and wonders why the Lord will not intervene and save His people. But God tells him that things are going to get even worse. Poor Habakkuk finds himself sandwiched between the tyranny of the Assyrians and the even greater wrath of the approaching Babylonians.

Yet at the end of the book the prophet summarizes, "Though the fig tree does not bud and there are no grapes on the vines, though the olive crop fails and the fields produce no food, though there are no sheep in the pen and no cattle in the stalls, yet I will rejoice in the Lord, I will be joyful in God my Saviour" (verses 17, 18).

But how was Habakkuk able to conclude that? I think it was because eventually he was able to grasp the complete story. Even though the Babylonians would arrive with great violence, God promised the prophet that He would ultimately destroy them, and that kept Habakkuk's hope alive.

We know the full story. Although we may also be trapped between terrible violence and moral corruption all around, and the prophetic promise is that even worse looms ahead, God has told us the end of the story. He is sovereign over all of history. So we have every reason for hope.

2. I face a future of hope because my Father is present. "And surely I am with you always, to the very end of the age" (Matt. 28:20).

I have always remembered a college friend remarking, "When God seems far away, who's moved?" It's so true. We get busy and then think that He has gone somewhere. Of course He hasn't gone anywhere. He's still right with us, longing for communion.

Because we live such hectic lives, we often lose touch of the reality of His presence. However, Brother Lawrence found a way of maintaining contact with God in spite of the rush around him. He lived in the 1600s, and having studied other people's ideas of how to have a relationship with God, he found them confusing and unhelpful. Out of his deep desire to live completely for God, he decided that he was going to act as though only he and God existed in the world. In a letter he explained how "at all times, every hour, every minute, even in the height of my business, I drove away from my mind everything that was capable of interrupting my thought of God" (*The Practice of the Presence of God,* p. 32).

Brother Lawrence tried to make practicing the presence of God the habit of his entire life. He wasn't trying to avoid people or reality. Rather, his intention was to let God's presence be so real and strong in his mind that God's way of thinking and living would shape how he interacted with everyone around him.

When in prayer, Brother Lawrence would often think of himself in different ways. In the following quotation he describes how he did this and its ultimate purpose. "Sometimes I considered myself before Him as a poor criminal at the feet of his judge; at other times I beheld him in my heart as my Father, as my God…. Sometimes I considered myself there, as a stone before a carver, whereof he is to make a statue; presenting myself thus before God, I desire Him to make His perfect image in my soul, and make me entirely like Himself" (*ibid.,* pp. 31-37).

Remaining conscious of God's presence is something I have often struggled with. I also find it too easy to become distracted by the pace of life, and eventually conclude that God has abandoned me. But one day God showed me just how close He really is.

I was standing on the majestic Chain Bridge, hanging over the railings, as the Danube River slowly passed beneath. I was excited to be in Budapest for the first time, but the anxiety of recent weeks had been overwhelming.

As I walked back to my hotel I ached inside. Without a single idea of how to ease the pressure, I decided to fast for the next 24 hours. Whatever the solution was, I knew that God was the only one who could help.

Sitting on my couch, I stared around the room with tears in my eyes. As Christians we believe that God is with us. But sometimes, perhaps unconsciously, we imagine Him floating around us like some mysterious vapor. Jesus is more tangible to grasp because we've seen pictures of Him in Sabbath school, and we can just about visualize Him walking around Israel. But God the Father and the Holy Spirit are harder to grasp.

But then I saw, across the other side of the room, a chair facing me. Perhaps God was sitting there? The thought both amazed and horrified me. I was amazed by the concept that my Father could actually be with me, here in my room, but then horrified to realize that I could allow myself to descend into such despair when the God who loves me so much, was so close.

Then another thought struck me. Right next to me, just at the end of my couch, was another chair. Perhaps God could be sitting there?

My eyes grew larger as the possibility sunk in. Again amazement filled me at the possible closeness of His presence, alternating with horror at my own faithlessness. As I sat and stared at that chair, I realized that if God was indeed sitting in it, our knees would almost be touching.

He's close enough to hold my hand, I marveled.

Words that were crystal clear shot back in my mind, taking me off guard. *No,* came the insistence, *I'm close enough to carry you.*

Realizing that God is always present brings peace. God is with us now. He has named himself Emmanuel, emphasizing His promise never to leave us, even "to the very end of the age" (Matt. 28:20). And the reality of God's presence brings hope.

3. I face a future of hope because my Father is involved in it. " 'For I know the plans I have for you,' declares the Lord, 'plans to prosper you and not to harm you, plans to give you hope and a future. Then you will call upon me and come and pray to me, and I will listen to you. You will seek me and find me when you seek me with all your heart' " (Jer. 29:11-13).

One Friday evening during my ministerial internship God confronted me with His involvement in my life. I decided to walk to my senior pastor's house for our weekly Bible study group. It was quite dark, and I was following an unused railway track. The tree branches from either side were almost closing me in. Suddenly I stopped dead in my tracks as a voice seemed to come out of nowhere.

"Be still, and know that I am God."

Rooted to the spot, I stared instinctively upward.

"What am I supposed to know?" I asked. It was the only thought that came into my head.

"I have plans for you," the voice said. *"Plans for you to prosper."*

And that was it. But I felt overwhelmed with joy.

When I arrived at the house and walked into the living room, people stared at me in astonishment.

"What happened to you?" they asked hesitantly. I just couldn't stop smiling. (I knew those words were a Bible text, and to my embarrassment it took me two days to find them in Jeremiah 29:11-13.)

I cannot tell you what an inspiration those words have been to me throughout my ministry. Everywhere I look it seems that so many people are aching to hear such a promise of reassurance. So whenever I have the chance, I write that text in a card, hoping that the promise will mean as much to the recipient as it has to me. When my wife and I got married, we decided to have the reference in Jeremiah inscribed inside our wedding rings as constant reminders of God's promises to us. And we even have the text on a wall that is the first thing people see when they walk through our front door. We want everyone who comes into our home to know that God's wonderful plans are for their lives too.

Jeremiah wrote his words to people living in exile. In the verses at the beginning of the chapter he lays out the foundation for why they should hope in God.

First, God tells His people that they should keep hope alive because their situation is not the result of chance or unpredictable evil: He has been actively involved from the beginning. For God himself says, "I carried [Judah] into exile from Jerusalem to Babylon" (Jer. 29:4). Though evil seems to surround them, Judah has never left the protection of His hands.

Second, God tells His people that they should keep hope alive because He can intervene within their present difficulties: "Also, seek the peace and prosperity of the city to which I have carried you into exile. Pray to the Lord for it, because if it prospers, you too will prosper" (verse 7).

Third, God tells His people that they should keep hope alive because He is going to bring an end to their exile at a specific time. "This is what the Lord says: 'When seventy years are completed for Babylon, I will come to you and fulfil my gracious promise to bring you back to this place'" (verse 10).

74

We too are in exile. But the future is bright. For we have exactly the same reasons not to lose our hope—God is still involved, working out His plans. And at a specific time our exile will end.

4. I face a future of hope because our Father is very great. "Where were you when I laid the earth's foundation? Tell me, if you understand" (Job 38:4).

I think that the ending of Job is amazing. After his friends have hogged the stage for almost the entire book, God's voice booms from the sky and silences everyone. "Who is this that darkens my counsel with words without knowledge?" (verse 2). Without pausing, the Lord turns to Job and raises 50 jaw-dropping questions.

God asks him if he was there when He made the earth and if he can control the constellations or organize the lives of the animals. The questions go on and on. After the last question Job replies, "I am unworthy—how can I reply to you? I put my hand over my mouth. I spoke once, but I have no answer—twice, but I will say no more" (Job 40:4, 5).

But the Lord is not finished. Beginning again, He poses another round of questions about the behemoth and the leviathan.

God never answers any of the "why" questions of Job's friends, but rather paints a picture of His unparalleled greatness through the works of His creation. After this, Job does not need any answers: "Surely I spoke of things I did not understand, things too wonderful for me to know. You said, 'Listen now, and I will speak; I will question you, and you shall answer me.' My ears had heard of you but now my eyes have seen you. Therefore I despise myself and repent in dust and ashes" (Job 42:3-6).

An overwhelming picture of divine magnificence has eclipsed any need for explanations.

This story reveals a fascinating paradox. Hope and encouragement can spring from the realization that we know so little. Instinctively we try to find hope through trying to know everything, and we become discouraged when we cannot find the answers for which we are searching. But sometimes God highlights our ignorance and inability to know so that we may realize that hope does not originate in "finding answers" but in a being vastly greater than ourselves.

"Divine inspiration asks many questions which the most profound scholar cannot answer. These questions were not asked that we might answer them, but to call our attention to the deep mysteries of God and to teach us that our wisdom is limited; that in the surroundings of our daily life there are many things beyond the comprehension of finite minds; that the judgments and purposes of God are past finding out. His wisdom is unsearchable.

"Sceptics refuse to believe in God because with their finite minds they cannot comprehend the infinite power by which He reveals Himself to men. But God is to be acknowledged more from what He does not reveal of Himself than from that which is open to our limited comprehension. Both in divine revelation and nature, God has given to men mysteries to command their faith. This must be so. We may be ever searching, ever inquiring, ever learning, and yet there is an infinity beyond" (Ellen G. White, *Testimonies,* vol. 8, p. 261).

How big is your God? I think that if we were to catch a glimpse of the unsurpassed greatness of God the way Job did, our questions may yet remain unanswered, but we would be filled with an inexplicable and joyous hope.

A God Like No Other

Hope is found in a person. This unexpectedly became real to me during a dreadful day of rioting that swept the Sri Lankan capital, Colombo.

It was at the time of the annual all-island swimming competition, and a couple friends and I were going down to the pool to warm up. But before we had jumped out of our car, the pool attendant rushed up to us. Pointing behind us, he announced, "Pool closed. Curfew at 2:00 p.m." We turned around and looked. Two gigantic plumes of smoke slowly wound their way into the sky.

Instantly we knew what had happened. The racial tensions between the two dominant ethnic groups on the island had boiled over. Now the larger group was burning the others' homes and factories. After we raced back to school, I picked up my bike and quickly pedaled home. As I neared our mission compound, more columns of smoke billowed into the air close to the house.

The fires across the city burned all day long. During the afternoon, men, women, and children suddenly began clambering over our 10-foot-high wall. One old man even tried to heave his fridge over with him. Then came the sound of shouting, breaking glass, and finally the crackle of fire as people looted the shops next to our compound and set them alight. I stood on top of our wall, trying to put out fires with our garden hose. The most I could do was to stop the flames from getting closer. Inside our house huddled about 25 shaking and sobbing people.

Toward evening another group wanted refuge in our home. To avoid being seen by those around the compound, my mother led them to our front door, with everyone walking doubled up below a shorter four-foot-high section of our wall. But a lookout on a nearby building site spotted them. A few hours later we received a message that the rioters would burn our house that night.

But we were told not to worry. Some friends had a little influence with the local police, who scheduled an extra army patrol around our block. They also located an armed guard for our door. Not too confident about the arrangements, we phoned the British High Commission, which was only a mile and a half down the road. However, they said that the city was in such chaos that they could do nothing to help. Two armed police officers arrived, but both were scared and had become quite drunk. The single bullet that each officer possessed did not give any of us much assurance.

That night my mother and two younger brothers climbed over a far wall into a neighbor's house. Our refugees, camped out in my bedroom, quietly and nervously talked among themselves. I lay down on a camping bed across the room from my father. Beside me we had a suitcase containing one set of clothes each and our passports. I slept in my clothes.

It was hard getting to sleep. My eyes stung from the continuous smoke and were quite red. Outside, our lawn was no longer green but was now a macabre gray, blanketed by a thick layer of ash.

Randomly opening my Bible, I glanced at the page and saw, "He who dwells in the shelter of the Most High will rest in the shadow of the Almighty. I will say of the Lord, 'He is my refuge and my fortress, my God, in whom I trust'" (Ps. 91:1, 2).

I hadn't reached the third verse before my father, on his bed on the other side of the room, said, "Gavin, I want to read you something." He began, "'He who dwells in the shelter of the Most High . . .'" I couldn't believe it! It was as if God had opened both His arms and had wrapped them tightly around me.

I didn't tell my father that we had been reading the same text, feeling that it was God's secret to me, just between just the two of us.

Thirteen years later I needed a children's story at church, so I told them how God spoke to me through Psalm 91. "And what is the probability," I asked the children, "that both my father and I would turn to the same passage at the same time?"

"Enormous," boomed one of the children, as if she was stating the blatantly obvious. The congregation laughed. But she was right.

I decided to tell the same story the following week at my other church. My mother was visiting from Pakistan, where she and my father were serving as missionaries, and so I prefaced the story by saying that I had never mentioned the incident to anyone in my family. However, as I finished, I noticed my mother beaming all over with her hand raised.

"There is another part to that story that you don't know," she began. "When I took your brothers over the wall to that neighbor's house that night, I opened my Bible and read to them 'He who dwells in the shelter of the Most High . . .'"

I don't remember what children's hymn we sang next—only that a rather large lump in my throat refused to let a single word escape. Here I was about to expound the words of God to my congregation, when the God of the words expounded in a mysterious way an unexpected word about Himself to me. It was a word about His control over events, a word about His presence and involvement in my life, a word about His greatness and a lot more besides.

I tell this story every time I have the opportunity. And I never get bored by it, because it reminds us that even though we may enter fiery crucibles and are not sure what is happening, we can still have hope. For God Himself is our unshakeable hope, and He is with us.

Father,

> *Wherever I go, in whatever circumstances I find myself in, teach me to see You.*

> *Fill my mind and heart with a longing for You, not just for the things You can do for me.*

> *May You always be my hope—an unshakable, immovable God on whom I can utterly depend.*

In Jesus' name, amen.

CHAPTER 8

Faith—in the Invisible God

"Now faith is being sure of what we hope for and
certain of what we do not see."
Hebrews 11:1

Why Faith Matters

The author of Hebrews makes a disturbing declaration: "Without faith it is impossible to please God, because anyone who comes to him must believe that he exists and that he rewards those who earnestly seek him" (Heb. 11:6).

Jesus echoes those strong words about a lack of faith. Matthew regularly records Him chastising people for faithlessness, something He started from the very beginning of His ministry. In the Sermon on the Mount Jesus laments, "O you of little faith" (Matt. 6:30). His closest followers are not immune from His chiding. In the middle of a storm He questions His disciples, "You of little faith, why are you so afraid?" (Matt. 8:26). When Peter began to sink in another storm, He asks, "You of little faith, why did you doubt?" (Matt. 14:31). Later Jesus interrupts their discussion to say, "You of little faith, why are you talking among yourselves about having no bread?" (Matt. 16:8). Christ seems quite harsh.

By contrast, He regularly commended the presence of genuine faith. Again, if we just consider the stories in Matthew, Jesus expresses astonishment at the faith of a Roman centurion (Matt. 8:10). He then voices His affirmation that faith was the reason for the healing of the paralytic (Matt. 9:2), a sick woman (verse 22), the two blind men (verses 29, 30), and the daughter possessed by demons (Matt. 15:28).

Jesus was deliberately raising the visibility of faith because it determined whether the power of God could enter and transform their lives. As the disciples discovered firsthand, their failure to cast out an evil spirit was "because you have so little faith" (Matt. 17:20). Indeed, the whole town of Nazareth suffered as Jesus "did not do many miracles there because of

79

their lack of faith" (Matt. 13:58). The Savior talked tough on faith because He knew full well that faithlessness and the transforming power of heaven were completely incompatible.

It's the same today. Our ability to stay on the path to the Shepherd's house, and for our spiritual lives to reflect more clearly the character of Jesus (or not), still depends on faith.

What Is Faith?

Before we go any further, we need to define faith. The book of Hebrews gives a simple definition: "Now faith is being sure of what we hope for and certain of what we do not see" (Heb. 11:1). But living a life of such assurance is not as simple as it looks. *How* are we to be certain about things invisible? We may feel confident of an unseen God when things are going well, but when crucibles enter our lives they can undermine our confidence in a God beyond our seeing. Crucibles by their very nature cause us to doubt and even despair of a kind and loving Father, for when we are in the middle of the crucible we rarely perceive any evidence of His intervention on our behalf. We may pray and pray, but nothing appears to make any difference. All we may see is blackness.

Learning to See in the Dark

Many people claim that faith is a leap in the dark. What they mean is that faith is a jump into the unknown. But that is not how the Bible describes it. Hebrews again maintains that Moses was able to stand against the wrath of Pharaoh and the whole nation of Egypt, leading Israel out of slavery, because he "saw him who is invisible" (verse 27). Faith sees clearly, and the impact of such faith on our lives can be incredible. "This is the way in which Moses succeeded. He lived as seeing Him who is invisible, and was therefore able to count the reproaches of Christ greater riches than the treasures of Egypt. If men would live in this way, we should see their faces aglow with the glory of God; for they would be viewing the glory of the eternal, and by beholding, would be transformed into the image of Christ" (Ellen G. White, in *Signs of the Times,* Jan. 9, 1893).

So how does faith "see" clearly, even under pressure? How can it perceive the face of Christ so thoroughly that we can be transformed into His image? Here are two ways that faith perceives the "invisible" Jesus.

First, faith sees the face of Jesus because faith is shaped by the words of God.

David declares, "Your word is a lamp to my feet and a light for my path" (Ps. 119:105). God's Word always bring light, enabling us to view reality as heaven does, rather than how we feel it. So when we are in the middle of the crucible, the light of God's words helps us to determine the truth about our situation despite our turbulent feelings and Satan's temptations to doubt God's love for us.

I will never forget the time I had my own faithlessness in God's promises ruthlessly exposed. The process of recognizing my problem and learning what to do about it took roughly a year.

I think it started when I stood talking to a missionary couple in the middle of a deserted school hall. We had just finished an evangelistic meeting, and I was asking for some advice. Two days before, I had encountered something I could never have imagined. A young man I had been talking to had suddenly become angry and violent. All I had done was ask him about his relationship with God. He was possessed by evil spirits.

The missionary woman talked about her service in the Caribbean.

"One night three big young men broke into our house," she began. "All of the men in our house froze as the intruders appeared with big baseball bats. No one knew what to do, and these youths looked angry. I stood there and pointed directly at them and cried, 'In the name of Jesus, get out!'"

It would have been quite a sight to see, as she is about five feet tall and quite petite.

"And you know what?" she continued. "Those youths spun around on their heels and ran out as fast as they could." She looked me in the eye and added soberly, "You must always remember that there is power in the name of Jesus."

Finishing our conversation, I loaded all the evangelistic supplies into my beat-up Volkswagen Golf. Wearily I sat down in the driver's seat and put the key in the ignition.

"We are going to get you now."

I stared wide-eyed through the windshield, hardly able to believe what I had heard. The words were clear and their demonic origin unmistakable. Turning on my music, I drove off while trying to pretend that I had imagined it all. But it wasn't my imagination. It was clear that Satan's angels were angry that I was helping this man to become free from their control, and now they were after me. Turning up the music as high as I could tolerate it, I began to sing along with it.

Arriving home, I found the silence of an empty house too much, so I put on a CD loud enough so that I could hear it upstairs in my office. Every now and again some of the words to the songs would suddenly break into my consciousness. "There is strength in the name of the Lord; there is power in the name of the Lord." The lyrics were clearly echoing my earlier conversation.

Finally I climbed into my bed and fell asleep.

Suddenly I awoke with a jolt, gasping for air. It was as though my throat was being squeezed tightly and I could not get any breath. I was choking. Instantly the thoughts of a few hours earlier flashed into my mind. "In name of Jesus, get out," I spluttered as forcefully as I could. Immediately the pressure around my throat vanished.

At the very moment I called out to Jesus, the satanic power attacking me fell powerless.

However, as I lay in the darkness, my fears piled on top of each other until I was so terrified that I couldn't move. I knew that the evil spirits were real and that they were there or had just been there. What would come next?

I prayed out loud and tried to sing every hymn I could remember, but nothing made me feel better. The whole experience left me puzzled—I was a pastor and knew all about faith and confidence in God, but I felt stripped of every protection. I dared not even turn over in bed, as my imagination pictured all sorts of things that could be creeping up behind me. So much for faith.

After an hour of singing, my voice was hoarse, and it was not working anyway. Finally at 3:00 a.m. I grabbed my phone and dialed the number of a fellow minister. His wife answered, and as I shakingly related what had just happened, she replied, "OK. I will hand the phone over to John for him to talk with you, and I will start praying."

We talked for more than an hour, reviewing God's promises together, but they all sounded so remote. My fears had outgrown even the greatest of God's promises. Eventually, though, I began to feel some comfort and, after a closing prayer, fell asleep exhausted.

For the next six months I would be fast asleep in bed, only suddenly to wake up instantly terrified. A sense of evil always seemed to hang around my bedroom, and I felt totally helpless to do anything about it. My fear would not go away.

What made things worse was that my daily devotions began to fade. I prayed and studied my Bible only when necessary. It wasn't that I was failing to believe, but rather the opposite. Everything was just too real. Whenever I began to read or pray, it reminded me of this unseen reality, this great battle that I couldn't see, and my fears would come flooding back. I had thought I was a strong pastor, but now I felt as if I were made out of straw.

It was a number of months before a solution to my faith problem arrived. I was facing another tough experience alone. Because I was single, it was particularly difficult, because I had no one close by to talk to. I prayed to my Father, but right then I really wanted to speak to a human being.

"Father, I really need someone to talk to!" I pleaded, not really expecting an answer. Suddenly a blunt reply flashed back into my mind: *You can't have anyone.*

It stunned and confused me. "Well," I began, "how am I supposed to get what I need?"

What I am going to describe next had never happened to me before. I saw a picture. It was a portrayal of the resurrected Jesus. It was not an image with details, but I just knew that Jesus was standing in front of me, and that He was the one who sits at the right hand of the Father. His arms were outstretched toward me, with His hands cupped together. I sensed that in those hands was everything I could ever need.

"Why do you think that Jesus had to die?" the Holy Spirit probed. "So you could be miserable? You have got to appropriate what you need by faith."

I stood thinking for a moment. More than anything else I wanted peace and joy. In my mind I reached into those outstretched hands and took out "peace" and "joy." Instantly the most wonderful peace and joy filled me.

As the rest of the day continued, anytime I felt my fear creeping back I would mentally reach out again and take what I needed from those outstretched hands.

The experience lasted only a day, but in those hours I began to learn something so important that I would willingly go through all those months of fear again if I knew it was the only way to learn this lesson.

I began to realize the truth about the Resurrection. It is a fact of history beyond a doubt. But what the Resurrection achieved is also beyond a doubt. The Bible announces that when Jesus rose into heaven there took place a joyful coronation as heaven proclaimed Him king of our world. At the same time, the gifts of the Holy Spirit for the building up of His body, the church, were lavishly poured out to us. As Paul declares: "This is why it says: 'When he ascended on high, he led captives in his train and gave gifts to men'" (Eph. 4:8).

My faith problem was that while I knew that God had gifts for me, the knowledge made no impact personally—not at all. I hoped that God would protect me, but as I lay in bed night after night, I was never really sure if He would. After all, my guardian angel hadn't seemed very active that previous night.

However, during the next few weeks a new pattern of thinking began to develop in my mind. If the Bible's account of the resurrection was a fact, so must be the many promises of God's protection. The whole thing had a simple logic to it. It was not a question of how I felt, but a question of the truth about God and the resurrection of Jesus—and that resurrection truth, based squarely on Scripture, had to shape my reality.

Later, whenever I woke up feeling scared, I would think to myself, *No, in the Bible God has promised to protect me—and the Resurrection guarantees it. I can't see an angel, but I have prayed for protection and by faith. I believe that God is there and that He is strong enough to deal with anything. Father, please cocoon me in Your love and protection.* Then I would turn over in bed, something I had struggled to do for many months, confident that my protection was a certainty.

God does not make promises only for us to wonder if they are true. Yet unless we fully believe that they are, the blessings that accompany those promises will remain stacked on the shelves of heaven. Then it's like holding a gift voucher without ever trading it in for the real thing.

Jesus promised, "I will do whatever you ask in my name, so that the Son may bring glory to the Father. You may ask me for anything in my name, and I will do it" (John 14:13, 14). And the challenging thing for us is that He really means it. Then when we act on His promises, we begin to see clearly.

Second, faith sees the face of Jesus because faith is empowered by the Spirit of God through prayer. When we are in the crucible, God's words remind us of what is real. However, if mere knowing would change our lives, then perhaps we would all have been fully transformed a long time ago. Alongside a knowledge of God's words that shape our faith in Jesus, there also needs to be the power of the Spirit to give our faith legs—to enable us to trade in the promises for the real thing.

The struggle of knowing God's promises but failing to see the promises bear fruit was certainly a frustration for the disciples. To their surprise, they found themselves dealing with a demon-possessed man from whom the evil spirits stubbornly refused to leave. Eventually Jesus returned with Peter, James, and John from the Mount of Transfiguration. "When they came to the crowd, a man approached Jesus and knelt before him. 'Lord, have mercy on my son,' he said. 'He has seizures and is suffering greatly. He often falls into the fire or into the water. I brought him to your disciples, but they could not heal him.'

"'O unbelieving and perverse generation,' Jesus replied, 'how long shall I stay with you? How long shall I put up with you? Bring the boy here to me.' Jesus rebuked the demon, and it came out of the boy, and he was healed from that moment.

"Then the disciples came to Jesus in private and asked, 'Why couldn't we drive it out?'

"He replied, 'Because you have so little faith. I tell you the truth, if you have faith as small as a mustard seed, you can say to this mountain, "Move from here to there" and it will move. Nothing will be impossible for you'" (Matt. 17:14-20).

Ellen White offers an interesting commentary on the incident. "In order to succeed in such a conflict they must come to the work in a different spirit. Their faith must be strengthened by fervent prayer and fasting, and humiliation of heart. They must be emptied of self, and be filled with the Spirit and power of God. Earnest, persevering supplication to God in faith—faith that leads to entire dependence upon God, and unreserved consecration to His work—can alone avail to bring men the Holy Spirit's aid in the battle against principalities and powers, the rulers of the darkness of this world, and wicked spirits in high places" (*The Desire of Ages,* p. 431).

The disciples intellectually believed the promises of Jesus, but their knowledge was not yet faith. To be sure, they had cast out spirits at other times, but they now faced a new situation that demanded fresh faith. And such a life-transforming faith could be empowered only from heaven.

The need of such heavenly empowerment was impressed upon me during a time when I was again struggling—even to pray. I had become extremely frustrated with my work, and somehow my frustration had redirected itself toward God. I had become so irritated that the very idea of prayer made me angry, a strange and surprising reaction for someone who has spent his whole ministry teaching about its importance and power. It was a lot of effort just kneeling down, for inside I was battling with a God whom I believed had brought me purposely to failure. I didn't like His methods, but my own antagonism just made me weaker.

I literally had to take a break from work, and went with my wife to a summer house in the country. It was there that I decided that I must force myself to pray. Day by day as I persevered in prayer before God, I began to sense a gradual restoration of His power in my life. By the end of those two weeks the depression that I had struggled with for at least four years had vanished completely.

In case I would be tempted to think that I was imagining God's teaching, two days later He allowed me to see the same problem in the life of a friend. As we began talking, I noticed that a great burden seemed to crease her whole face. Soon she began sharing her profound discouragement. Her depression was so strong that she had ordered some pills from the doctor. Strangely, the more she talked, the more surprised I became. I thought I was listening to myself speaking just a few weeks before.

"You know this is a supernatural battle," I offered. "How's your prayer life?"

Glancing down sadly, she replied, "I haven't been able to talk to God for a long time."

Then I began to share with her my recent experience, telling that I hadn't been able to pray either. Sure, I had prayed the "official" prayer for the beginning of each day and a quick one at night, and yes, even some short ones during the day. But they were not prayers of real faith that could heal the aching of my soul.

We talked about faith and prayer and the restoring power of the Holy Spirit. The more I shared, the more I could hear my own voice echoing back to me. Yes, God had sent me to my friend, but the Lord was forcing me to listen to my own words—to remind me that it was He that had been at work those past few weeks.

As I left, my friend said, "I think God sent you to me tonight." And I couldn't help agreeing.

A couple weeks later I visited her again. The first thing I noticed when I walked into her apartment was her glowing face. She had become totally transformed.

Jesus also knew the power that results only from communion. "Behold the Son of God bowed in prayer to His Father! Though He is the Son of God, He strengthens His faith by prayer, and by communion with heaven gathers to Himself power to resist evil and to minister to the needs of men" (Ellen G. White, *The Acts of the Apostles* [Mountain View, Calif.: Pacific Press Pub. Assn., 1911], p. 56).

Faith, then, sees Jesus when the words of God are clear, and the power of God is within us.

Beware Presumption

In our discussion of faith I think it is important to be alert to something that often masquerades as faith. Particularly when we are in the crucible, if we are not aware of this substitute it can cause us considerable confusion.

I first became aware of presumption as an overzealous teenager. It was the year that Halley's Comet returned, and as it was a once-in-a-lifetime event not to be missed, I determined not to miss it.

While the comet was visible for a number of weeks in varying intensity, I had decided to wait until the newspapers said it was the very best time for viewing. I was in the middle of some really important exams, and I didn't want to be getting up at 4:00 in the morning unless the comet was going to be looking good. Finally the night came when I set my alarm at the auspicious time, and went to bed.

When my alarm went off, I shot out of bed and headed up a rather rickety ladder on the side of our water tower. Until that point I had not glanced at the night sky, because I wanted to wait until I was in the perfect place at the perfect time. Finally it was the perfect time, and I was in the perfect place. So I looked up. Scarcely able to believe my eyes, I found myself staring into clouds. As far as I could see, the cloud layer was thick and heavy. I had forgotten one small detail: it was monsoon season in Asia.

I was downcast only for a moment. Then I remembered the words that Jesus told to His disciples: "If you have faith as small as a mustard seed, you can say to this mulberry tree, 'Be uprooted and planted in the sea,' and it will obey you" (Luke 17:6). I thought to myself, *These are just a few puffy clouds. I know my God has the power to move them.* So I bowed my head and prayed, "God, I know You have all the power in the universe, and You can easily move these clouds. Please, will You move them so I can see the comet? In Jesus' name, amen." In great assurance of the power of faith, I looked up. But the same thick cloud obscured the sky.

It was then that I became a little worried. Perhaps my faith wasn't very strong. Maybe God needed more time to get the wind to blow the clouds away. So I went back down to my bedroom and decided to give Him another 20 minutes. Surely that would be plenty of time.

After praying some more prayers of faith and belief in God's power, I clambered back up the rickety ladder to the roof. Hardly able to contain my anticipation, I looked up. But there above me was the very same thick monsoon cloud that had been there 20 minutes earlier. I was stunned. I'm certain that I was the only person in the whole world who never saw Halley's Comet that year.

Presumption is assuming that God will do something simply because we think He is able. We don't have to be arrogant to be presumptuous. We need only to be thinking outside the boundaries of His promises. And in my case, I have not yet been able to find a promise of God that offers to move clouds for my entertainment.

Real faith always has a foundation for it. If you can quote its basis, then you can claim its promise. So if you find yourself struggling with any issue, pray for God's guidance as you search His Word. Look for as many verses as you can that help to define reality as God sees it, and that present His promises of help. Then morning and evening, pray that His Holy Spirit will allow His Word to shape your thoughts and feelings so that when you walk through the crucible, you may still be able to live out the life of God's kingdom on earth.

Faith Is the Door to Home

Here's a final yet critical thought about the faith that God is looking for in us today. When Israel failed to enter the Promised Land after griping about the giants that roamed there, they came to a crisis of faith (Heb. 3:19). God had clearly said that He was giving them the land, but their eyes persuaded them that it could not be possible. Then things began to deteriorate as the faithless people turned on Moses and Aaron. "But the whole assembly talked about stoning them. Then the glory of the Lord appeared at the Tent of Meeting to all the Israelites. The Lord said to Moses, 'How long will these people treat me with contempt? How long will they refuse to believe in me, in spite of all the miraculous signs I have performed among them?'" (Num. 14:10, 11).

As a result, the whole nation found itself condemned to the discipline of the wilderness for 40 years. When the people finally entered under Joshua, they did so because of their faith. At the beginning of the book of Joshua, God told Israel's leader to prepare the people to inhabit the land He had promised them. So Joshua tells them to get ready. Only when they are standing in their traveling clothes does the Lord explain what to do next. He commanded the priests to stand in the Jordan River. "Now the Jordan is at flood stage all during harvest. Yet as soon as the priests who carried the ark reached the Jordan and their feet touched the water's edge, the water from upstream stopped flowing. It piled up in a heap" (Joshua 3:15, 16). To walk into a flooded river was either stupid or inspired. In this case, it was according to God's Word. As a response to their faith in His words, the waters parted and the whole nation entered the Promised Land.

I must admit that I am disturbed by Ellen White's reflection—written many years ago—that "it was not the will of God that Israel should wander forty years in the wilderness. . . . In like manner, it was not the will of

God that the coming of Christ should be so long delayed and His people should remain so many years in this world of sin and sorrow. But unbelief separated them from God. As they refused to do the work which He had appointed them, others were raised up to proclaim the message" (Ellen G. White, *The Great Controversy* [Mountain View, Calif.: Pacific Press Pub. Assn., 1911], p. 458).

Could we all still be here, not just because the prophecies haven't all been fulfilled, or because heavenly beings still need to be convinced of the evilness of Satan, but because of our faithlessness in the words of God?

What I do know for certain is that those who are alive in the very last days will be alive by their faith. It won't be easy, for the crucible will be hot. But those who patiently "obey God's commandments and remain faithful to Jesus" (Rev. 14:12) will sing "a new song before the throne" (verse 3).

Faith matters a lot. It is faith that lifts our eyes to see the face of Jesus and brings heaven's miracles of transformation into our lives. And faith will then see us safely into the heavenly land.

Father,
> *I long for a faith that holds tightly to Your words, and keeps holding on until Your promises are realized.*
> *Grant me a fresh and living faith—a faith that does not rest upon what I see with my own physical eyes, but that clearly sees the face of Jesus.*
In Jesus' name, amen.

Praise—Faith in Action

"Rejoice in the Lord always. I will say it again: Rejoice!"
Philippians 4:4

I was flying back from Akureyri in the north of Iceland in a 50-seat twin-prop plane. As we had good weather, the captain announced that we would be flying lower than usual so that we could get a better view of the stunning scenery—craggy mountains covered with a thick layer of fresh snow.

I had just been reading a little book called *If,* by Amy Carmichael. At the end of her volume she describes how God's love is like an ever-flowing river. Day after day the waters pass by. It is always the same river, but the water—the love—is always new.

Thinking about this, I looked out my window. In the distance I noticed a huge waterfall cascading down one of the mountains. It was then I heard a whisper: "Such is My love."

The waterfall was quite a long way off, and considering its size, I knew that a huge amount of water must be flowing over the lip of the falls every second.

Where is all that water coming from? I wondered. I peered through the window for some time, but couldn't see its source.

Then I spotted it. Behind the waterfall, filling the horizon for as far as I could see, was an enormous glacier. The glacier was so large that I hadn't recognized what it was. There seemed to be enough water for the waterfall to continue flowing for hundreds and hundreds of years.

Suddenly I found myself in awe, engulfed inside an amazing metaphor. Is God's love for me really that big? Do I fail to see His love for me, not because it is so small, but because it is so large that I really have difficulty comprehending it? I struggled to take it all in. *Yes, God's love is really that big. Perhaps it is even bigger.*

It's at such moments—when we glimpse God's magnificence—that our hearts long to express themselves in praise. The problem is that praising God in the crucible is often challenging because we see little visible evidence of His goodness. So what then? Do we put praise on hold until a more convenient time? Can praise still be part of our experience during times of suffering as well?

In the chapter on faith we looked at how God's words repaint a picture of heaven's reality for us that has been warped by the pressures of the crucible. So if faith can exist and grow in the crucible, so can praise, for praise is simply the outward consequence of an inner trust.

But in the crucible, where we find little to remind us of God's love, praise is faith in action. Such praise is not just singing or making a noise in His direction. We can all sing endlessly without faith—even Christian hymns and songs—but the only thing that will happen after such endless singing is that our throats will become hoarse. I know, because I've done it more than once.

Praising God in the Crucible

Paul was someone who managed to show his faith through praise to God in the crucible. I can imagine him sitting at a small cramped desk under house arrest in Rome. Outside, guards chat with each other as the apostle wonders how long he has to live. He ponders the future for the moment, shakes his head, then scribbles energetically on the parchment in front of him a thought to his friends in Philippi: "Rejoice in the Lord always. I will say it again: Rejoice! Let your gentleness be evident to all. The Lord is near. Do not be anxious about anything, but in everything, by prayer and petition, with thanksgiving, present your requests to God. And the peace of God, which transcends all understanding, will guard your hearts and your minds in Christ Jesus" (Phil. 4:4-7).

He was not asking God, "Why is this happening to me?" Rather, Paul had somehow learned to eclipse his own troubles with glorious praise.

But how?

Let me suggest two important principles that can help us to foster faith through praise, even when we might be sitting in the depths of a crucible.

Principles for Praising God Under Pressure 1: Act Your Faith Despite Your Feelings

When Paul encourages the Philippians to rejoice, he urges them to rejoice "always." If we are to take his statement at face value, it must mean that we are called to rejoice at times that our feelings don't want to at all.

I think this must have been true for the Israelites. We must realize that as God led them into the land they had been dreaming about for years, He didn't take them to peaceful, open, fertile plains, stretching as far as their eyes could see. He led them to the very opposite. Their kind Father in heaven led them directly to one of the most fortified cities in a region, chockablock with pagan people armed to the teeth.

Then God said to the Israelite army, "I would like you to walk around those high and mighty walls, but do not even think about touching those swords by your sides. Actually, don't even talk. Go around the walls in silence. Take the whole nation one trip around the walls in silence, and then go back to your camp. Oh, yes, and you can do the same tomorrow, and the next day, and the next . . ."

You can imagine what the people on the Jericho walls were thinking: *What sort of battle is this? Are they out of their minds?* They would have been even more surprised if they had known that the Israelites didn't have a clue what was happening either. All the Israelites could see was one very big city with extremely thick walls—and they weren't allowed to talk.

Here, of course, was the point. The reason the people had to walk around the wall day after day was that it was only by repeatedly facing such an overwhelming task that they would realize that they could not possibly win the battle on their own.

Interesting isn't it? God sends His people to do a task that He knows they cannot do on their own. He makes them stare at the overwhelming problem day after day, in the hope that they will eventually realize that any victory will be completely on account of Him.

The Israelites must have started out with all sorts of feelings tumbling around inside. But after six days of looking at the opposition, their fear or overenthusiasm for battle had dissolved into a quiet trust in God. And this was what He was waiting for.

We could probably call this "last-resort faith." We put our faith in God's plan because He has painted us into a corner where we find ourselves forced to acknowledge that there is really only one option left—faith. It's a tough way to learn the importance of faith, but it is one that God uses regularly.

On the seventh day He tells the people to march around the wall seven times. During the final round, when the priests blow their trumpets, Joshua commands the people, "Shout! For the Lord has given you the city!" (Joshua 6:16). "When the trumpets sounded, the people shouted, and at the sound of the trumpet, when the people gave a loud shout, the wall collapsed; so every man charged straight in, and they took the city" (verse 20).

I have always wondered why the people had to shout. It's tempting to think that maybe the great noise caused a lot of vibration that led to the walls crumbling, or that it was to scare the people on the walls before the Israelites charged in to take the city.

But the word "shout" in the original Hebrew language is the same word that David uses in the Psalms when he calls the people to worship God: "Shout with joy to God, all the earth! Sing the glory of his name; make his praise glorious! Say to God, 'How awesome are your deeds! So great is your power that your enemies cringe before you. All the earth bows down to you; they sing praise to you, they sing praise to your name'" (Ps. 66:1-4).

The Old Testament's authors summon God's people to "shout for joy," because of the greatness of their God. They are to shout for joy, not just because they can see what He has done in the past, but also because He has promised to act for them in the future. That is why Joshua tells the people, "Shout! For the Lord has given you the city!"

Most of the time we praise God after He's done something nice for us. At Jericho God called His people to praise Him for His promise while they still had no evidence of its fulfillment. This is the key to praise that overcomes bewildering circumstances. It's living, breathing, speaking, acting, rejoicing according to what God has promised rather than only what we experience with our physical senses. The triumphant shout of praise was an act of faith. As the author of Hebrews tells us, it was "by faith the walls of Jericho fell" (Heb. 11:30).

Principles for Praising God Under Pressure 2: Practice It

Because praise in the crucible is often an act of faith contrary to our feelings and emotions, it is something that we must practice.

Mark Twain once said of getting rid of a bad habit that it "cannot be tossed out the window; it must be coaxed down the stairs a step at a time!" I think the same is also true in reverse. Good habits must be helped up the stairs into the mind and life one step at a time. It's just the same with the habit of praise.

Many consider Charles Haddon Spurgeon, a British pastor who lived in the 1800s, as one of the greatest preachers of all time. His weekly sermons literally sold by the ton. Among his writings is a book called *The Practice of Praise: How to Develop the Habit of Abundant, Continual Praise in Your Daily Life.* There he outlines three steps to practice praise from Psalm

145:7: "They shall eagerly utter the memory of Your abundant goodness, and shall shout joyfully of Your righteousness" (NASB).

The three steps are as follows:

1. Practice looking around you. "They shall eagerly utter the memory of Your abundant goodness." To remember God's great goodness means that we first have to notice it. If we do not look around us to see God's goodness, then we will have nothing to praise Him about.

What can we perceive in the physical world that reminds us of His goodness? Have we taken the time to observe the beauty and intricacy of His creation? Or have we noted the harmony of nature? But perhaps more important, what can we see in the spiritual world that makes us want to rejoice in Him? Have we observed the many blessings that our salvation has brought us or the steady development of the importance of prayer and grace among our churches? The more time we take to observe, the more we will see, and the more reason we will have to praise our Father.

2. Practice remembering what you have seen. Do we keep in mind what God has done in the Bible? Do we think about when He has intervened throughout our lives with His goodness? At our baptism; times spent with Him in nature; special Communion services; Sabbaths; providential meetings with people? Do we hold these things in our thoughts so that they become permanent markers on the path to remind us of His purposes for our lives?

3. Practice talking about it. "They shall eagerly utter." Like a bubbling stream or a fountain, we are called to allow praise for God's goodness to flow unrestrictedly from our mouths. As we do so, it encourages us and everyone around us.

Spurgeon gives five reasons we should talk at great length of God's goodness.

First, we should continually praise God because we cannot help it, for the truth of His goodness compels us to speak out.

Second, we should continually praise Him because within our culture a myriad voices seek to drown out any praises for God. Therefore, the more society protests against Him, the more we should speak out for Him.

Third, we should continually praise God as a witness to those who don't know Him. Praise is not primarily a private matter, but demands that someone be listening—both God, to whom the praise is directed, and our neighbors, who need to know that our God is real and that the Christian life is worth embracing.

Fourth, we should continually praise God to encourage fellow

Christians. Often those who are struggling feel intensely alone and conclude that they have no way out of their predicament. We can strengthen them through our praise.

Fifth, we should continually praise God to glorify Him—for He is indeed worthy of our honor and praise. Praise to God is an activity that the whole universe is constantly involved in. How then can we, who have been redeemed from eternal condemnation, praise him any less? (adapted from C. H. Spurgeon, *The Practice of Praise* [New Kensington, Pa.: Whitaker House, 1995]).

"Then let us educate our hearts and lips to speak the praise of God for His matchless love. Let us educate our souls to be hopeful and to abide in the light shining from the cross of Calvary" (Ellen G. White, *The Ministry of Healing,* p. 253).

The Powerful Consequences of Praise

Fyodor Dostoyvsky wrote, "Believe to the end, even if all men [go] astray and you [are] left the only one faithful; bring your offering even then and praise God in your loneliness." That's quite a powerful comment from someone who endured a mock execution before being sent to hard labor camp in Siberia. He suffered much. In prison, epilepsy caused him to foam at the mouth and convulse on the ground. Afterward the Russian authorities made him serve in the Siberian Regiment for five years. Would you have been able to continue praising God in such a situation?

Praise is powerful because it is able to transform our inner hurts and fears. I remember suddenly waking up in the middle of the night and within minutes began to feel overwhelmed by negative thoughts. The more I churned them over, the more paralyzed I felt. Eventually I got up and put on a CD of praise music and sang along with it for an hour. Peace eventually replaced the heaviness and fear that had been so overwhelming some minutes before.

The same thing happened the next night. Again I felt overwhelmed, and again I felt renewed as I focused my mind on praising God. Just recently my wife also awakened with a sense of fear. She told the evil presence she felt to leave in the name of Jesus but nothing happened. So she began to praise God. Immediately her fear vanished.

Sometimes our words can be expressions of truth, yet lack the power that comes through faith. But as my wife expressed her words of faith directly to Christ, the power of God came and strengthened her faith, and the evil spirit did not remain.

THE REFINER'S FIRE

When praise is filled with faith, it has the power to do amazing things. Consider how praise can transform in these two examples.

First, praise has the power to convict hearts of sin and to create a longing for a better life. After Paul and Silas were flogged, thrown into a Philippi prison, and had their legs secured in stocks, they began to sing. They must have been aching and bleeding all over, but somehow their hearts overflowed with joy. In the middle of one song an earthquake broke open the prison, and the jailer, thinking that they had certainly gone—and that he would be held responsible for their escape—drew his sword to kill himself. But suddenly Paul's voice rang out: "Stop! We are all here!"

Rather than thinking about the safety of all the prisoners, the official's first thought was of his spiritual condition: "The jailer called for lights, rushed in and fell trembling before Paul and Silas. He then brought them out and asked, 'Sirs, what must I do to be saved?'" (Acts 16:29, 30).

The praise from Paul and Silas might have brought the earthquake that opened their prison doors, but even much more important, the doors of the spiritual prison in which the jailer had been unknowingly trapped also swung open in an instant, and that night he and his whole family were saved.

When I read this story, I can't help wondering what affect faith-filled praise could have on those around me. What could happen if it came more often from my lips?

Second, praise has the power to repel the strongest enemy. It was perhaps surprising that we would find Paul and Silas singing in prison, but equally strange that we should find the Israelite army singing all the way to face one of the greatest enemies they had ever encountered.

When King Jehoshaphat heard that a vast army was headed toward Judah, he immediately proclaimed a fast, and everyone met in Jerusalem to ask God what to do. Before long, under the inspiration of the Holy Spirit, Jahaziel stood up and announced, "Listen, King Jehoshaphat and all who live in Judah and Jerusalem! This is what the Lord says to you: 'Do not be afraid or discouraged because of this vast army. For the battle is not yours, but God's. Tomorrow march down against them. They will be climbing up by the Pass of Ziz, and you will find them at the end of the gorge in the Desert of Jeruel. You will not have to fight this battle. Take up your positions; stand firm and see the deliverance the Lord will give you, O Judah and Jerusalem. Do not be afraid; do not be discouraged. Go out to face them tomorrow, and the Lord will be with you'" (2 Chron. 20:15-18).

I think I would have been tempted to draw up a backup plan. But not Jehoshaphat. "Early in the morning they left for the Desert of Tekoa. As they set out, Jehoshaphat stood and said, 'Listen to me, Judah and people of Jerusalem! Have faith in the Lord your God and you will be upheld; have faith in his prophets and you will be successful.' After consulting the people, Jehoshaphat appointed men to sing to the Lord and to praise him for the splendor of his holiness as they went out at the head of the army, saying: 'Give thanks to the Lord, for his love endures forever'" (verses 20, 21).

Judah's king urges them to have faith and to express it in song. The ending—as with the incident at Jericho—was inevitable. "As they began to sing and praise, the Lord set ambushes against the men of Ammon and Moab and Mount Seir who were invading Judah, and they were defeated. The men of Ammon and Moab rose up against the men from Mount Seir to destroy and annihilate them. After they finished slaughtering the men from Seir, they helped to destroy one another. When the men of Judah came to the place that overlooks the desert and looked toward the vast army, they saw only dead bodies lying on the ground; no one had escaped" (verses 22-24).

Israel's songs of faith-filled praise caught the attention of heaven, and God totally destroyed the enemy.

Eternal Optimism

Faith fills the heart with praise because faith gives the heart reason for optimism. *Time* magazine reported an interesting study on the effect of optimism in people's lives. Metropolitan Life, a life insurance company in the United States, hired 5,000 salespeople a year at a cost of $30,000 each. The problem was that half of the people dropped out by the end of their first year, and four out of five had quit by the end of the fourth year. The reason so many salespeople left was that selling life insurance involved having the door slammed in one's face repeatedly. With the obvious need to reduce training costs, the company wanted to know if it was possible to identify potential salespeople who would be less likely to drop out in the face of unpleasant circumstances.

Martin Seligman, a psychologist from the University of Pennsylvania, carried out an experiment among 15,000 of the company's new employees. All of them had taken two screening tests. The first was the company's regular screening exam, while the second was designed to measure optimism. Seligman discovered that those who scored high in optimism did best, even though some of them failed the company's regular screening exam. In fact, the optimists outsold the pessimists by 21 percent in the first year and 57 percent in the second. He concluded that one reason that some people succeed where others fail is that the successful people attribute their failings to something that they can change, rather than something that they are powerless to overcome (Nancy Gibbs, "The EQ Factor," *Time,* Oct. 2, 1995).

If this is true, then perhaps Christians should make the best life insurance salespeople the world has ever seen. Though the parallels to success in selling eternal life insurance are worth thinking about, I want to highlight that the Christian's foundation for optimism—and therefore his or her ability to overcome bewildering and hurting circumstances—should be the most secure that a person can imagine. Our ability to overcome failure and difficult situations is found in the unrivaled and unlimited power of the living God. As members of His family, we should be the most joyful, praise-filled people alive, no matter what life slams in our face.

Paul summarizes our basis for praise in spite of our surrounding crucibles: "If God is for us, who can be against us? He who did not spare his own Son, but gave him up for us all—how will he not also, along with him, graciously give us all things? . . . Christ Jesus, who died—more than that, who was raised to life—is at the right hand of God and is also interceding for us. Who shall separate us from the love of Christ? Shall trouble or hardship or persecution or famine or nakedness or danger or sword? . . . No, in all these things we are more than conquerors through him who loved us. For I am convinced that neither death nor life, neither angels nor demons, neither the present nor the future, nor any powers, neither height nor depth, nor anything else in all creation, will be able to separate us from the love of God that is in Christ Jesus our Lord" (Rom. 8:31-39).

What better reason could you think of for a song?

Father,
   Teach me to praise You at all times,
   To rejoice in You,
   Not just because of what You have done,
   But also because of what You have promised.
   Whether I am in the light, or in the dark,
   May Your peace guard my heart and mind.
   May I rejoice in You, because You are near.
In Jesus' name, amen.

CHAPTER 10

Meekness— Faith in the Justice of God

"If you are insulted because of the name of Christ, you are blessed, for the Spirit of glory and of God rests on you."
1 Peter 4:14

Perhaps the greatest challenge we face as Christians is that of being meek. Jesus' voice has rung out loudly through the centuries: "Blessed are the meek, for they will inherit the earth" (Matt. 5:5). Yet to be honest, it is the one quality of Jesus that I sense most lacking in my own life. The thought even tempts me with fear.

Such a fear is not without foundation. *Merriam-Webster's Collegiate Dictionary* defines "meek" as "enduring injury with patience and without resentment." And who wants to do that?

I remember a time that the need for meekness really hit me hard. During the early years of my career I had gone through a prolonged period of illness. When I first fell ill, I found myself in the isolation wing of the tropical diseases hospital in London with hardly enough energy to speak. It was then that I received a letter from another pastor criticizing both me and my work. It came with no prior warning, and copies of it seemed to have gone to everyone. Soon I received a summons to appear at the conference office to answer the allegations. As well as feeling bad because of my illness, I was also extremely hurt. Later it was hard not to speculate that the accusations had some role in the eventual stopping of my contract some time later.

How are we to respond in such situations? I can tell you what I did. I carefully filed the letter away. Then as soon as I began feeling better, I started making enquires into my legal standing regarding my employment. It was good to hear that I had a case to sue. My hurt certainly justified a financial reward.

But did it really? I wasn't coming close to even the dictionary definition ("enduring injury with patience and without resentment"), let alone a biblical definition, of "meek." I had to make a choice, in spite of my feelings, to live my life according to Scripture rather than my own sense of injustice.

My feelings of injury did not go away quietly. My first staff meeting after I had been reemployed provided a test. On the other side of the room during a break stood my letter writer, drinking orange juice. Yet more than a decade later I still remember it was orange juice. Again, I had to make a choice, for Scripture compelled me as the hurting one to initiate bridge-building (John 3:16; Matt. 5:23, 24). It wasn't easy. Finally I walked across, smiled, and shook his hand. And as I did so, the emotional weight of the previous months dissolved.

I would like to say that this was the end of the story. It was perhaps the conclusion of the public story, but I knew that I still had his letter filed in my cabinet. One day, I reminded myself, I might need it as ammunition in a future battle.

I think it was about three years later that I came across the letter again, and it triggered a real conflict inside me. I wanted to live like Christ, yet I felt that my desire to guard myself against future injustice was reasonable. After some minutes of thought I ripped up the letter and threw it in the trash bin.

The experience taught me a lot. Most important, it explained why meekness often has to struggle to be visible in much of our lives. Meekness threatens my pride and my ego. It can undermine my natural ambition for success. That is why meekness often fills me with dread. I want to be a success, and I want it on my terms. Consequently, I don't do very well at meekness.

The more I think about meekness, the more I find myself coming to the conclusion that this most difficult of graces is potentially the greatest hallmark of the Christian, for such a life is impossible to live without a total infilling of divine power.

You see, we can't fake meekness. While we might try, we'll always be exposed by a generation that is scouring the horizon for glimpses of authenticity. But this very fact gives me reason for hope. When we learn how to imitate Christlike meekness, I believe we will have the most powerful and compelling testimony to the truth that God really does exist, and that His power is at work among us.

Characteristics of the Meek

So what does this most difficult of graces look like? What does God want to see in us so that we can authentically reflect the character of Jesus?

I don't find this easy to explain, but let me try to build a picture with four different facets.

1. Meekness continually seeks grace and mercy for those who hurt you. The Bible tells us that Moses was the meekest man who ever lived (Num. 12:3; most newer English translations employ the word "humble," which does not carry exactly the connotations that "meek" does). But why was Moses considered to be meek?

As I read through his story, I see him doing something again and again—praying for rebellious people, praying that God will be merciful to them, even though their complaints are often aimed directly at him personally. Here are six occasions on which this happens.

First, the people complain that Moses is making life difficult for them (Num. 11:1-3). God then sends fire out of heaven and consumes some on the outskirts of the camp. What does Moses say? "That's right, God! Punish those who have rebelled." Not at all. "When the people cried out to Moses, he prayed to the Lord and the fire died down" (verse 2).

Second, jealousy consumes Moses' own relatives, and they began to criticize him (Num. 12). God then sees that it is just to punish Miriam with leprosy. Does Moses say, "I know this is hard, God, but we all know she deserved it"? Hardly! "So Moses cried out to the Lord, 'O God, please heal her!'" (verse 13).

Third, the people become so angry that they want to replace Moses as leader (Num. 13; 14) "Then Moses and Aaron fell facedown in front of the whole Israelite assembly gathered there" (Num. 14:5). As His people talk about stoning their leader, God suggests to Moses, "I will strike them down with a plague and destroy them, but I will make you into a nation greater and stronger than they" (verse 12). Beginning with the episode of the golden calf, this is the second time that God offers to kill all the troublemakers and start over with Moses. *Yes, God,* I would have thought, *perhaps You are finally right. Let's start over again.* But such an idea does not enter Moses' mind. Instead, he reminds God that He is loving and forgiving of sin (verse 18), so the Lord lavishes His forgiveness on the people once again.

Fourth, sometime later all of Moses' assistant leaders gang up against him (Num. 16). So what do you do when your closest supporters club together to launch a coup? "When Moses heard this, he fell facedown" (verse 4). As Korah then picks up courage to force the rebellion, God tells Moses and Aaron again, "'Separate yourselves from this assembly so I can put an end to them at once.' But Moses and Aaron fell facedown and cried out, 'O God, God of the spirits of all mankind, will you be angry with the entire assembly when only one man sins?'" (verses 20-22).

Fifth, because of Moses' prayers, God spares the people, but He does kill Korah and the leaders of the rebellion. But the people that Moses has just spared through his prayers immediately begin to blame him and Aaron for the deaths. Yet again God announces, "Get away from this assembly so I can put an end to them at once" (verse 45), but Moses intervenes between God's justice and the people as he and Aaron fall "facedown." As Moses prays, he commands his brother to run into the middle of the people and begin making atonement for them. A plague from God is beginning to break out on the people. "But Aaron offered incense and made atonement for them. He stood between the living and the dead, and the plague stopped" (verse 47, 48). *Can't Moses hear what the people are saying about him?* I have to wonder to myself.

Sixth, it seems that no matter what Moses does, the people still complain. Just as they are about to enter the Promised land, God decides to test them to see if they have learned anything more than their parents, whom He had barred from the land 40 years before (Num. 20). As the pillar of cloud deliberately stops in a waterless place, the people exclaim, "If only we had died when our brothers fell dead before the Lord" (verse 3). As soon as Moses hears them, he and his brother go from "the assembly to the entrance to the Tent of Meeting and [fall] facedown" (verse 6).

Moses spent 40 years praying for grace for people who didn't seem to care the slightest. Yet in the face of God's justice, justice that the whole universe could have rejoiced in, Moses pleaded for mercy and grace. More than once, he avoided the temptation to become the father of a new people at the expense of the rebellious Israelites. He was a true intercessor, reflecting the meekness of Christ.

Tragically, though, that meekness unexpectedly unraveled. Moses finally snapped and become angry at their behavior, and rather than speaking to the rock for water as God had asked, he hit it twice. Ironically, grace poured out to quench the thirst of the wicked, and Moses, the now not-so-meek, was barred from entering the Promised Land.

Meekness is a priceless commodity. Finding its strength on one's knees, it overcomes justice, even God's justice, with grace. Though the wicked people didn't know it, that grace was what ushered them into the Promised Land.

2. Meekness does loving actions for the rebellious. I remember crossing the Newbold College lawn during my first year as a student. As I walked I noticed a girl sitting on a wall chatting to her friend. But she was not an ordinary girl, for I knew that every Friday evening she was either out partying in town or getting drunk in the pub around the corner. *What a bad person,* I thought to myself.

Instantly a familiar text confronted me: "For God did not send his Son into the world to condemn the world, but to save the world through him" (John 3:17). I felt rightly humbled. God calls us not to criticize but to save. And "save" is an action word.

We noted that Moses interceded continuously for grace for the undeserving, but let's take this a little further, as we may be tempted to think that meekness only prays. However, meekness has hands and legs, too.

To see meekness in action, Jesus gives us the example of His Father. "You have heard that it was said, 'Love your neighbor and hate your enemy.' But I tell you: Love your enemies and pray for those who persecute you, that you may be sons of your Father in heaven. He causes his sun to rise on the evil and the good, and sends rain on the righteous and the unrighteous. If you love those who love you, what reward will you get? Are not even the tax collectors doing that? And if you greet only your brothers, what are you doing more than others? Do not even pagans do that? Be perfect, therefore, as your heavenly Father is perfect" (Matt. 5:43-48).

Perfection as defined by this passage is not just thinking nice thoughts about your enemies, but bringing them practical things for their good. The Father does not simply think nice thoughts about sinners who have hurt Him deeply—He sends them rain to quench their thirst and grow their crops. Jesus tells us the same—engage in loving actions toward those who oppose us; then we will truly reflect the Father's character. But these loving actions will often need to be done *as* people are rebelling against, criticizing, plotting, or undermining us. Love, if it is godly love, will often have to love under pressure.

3. Meekness initiates reconciliation. We may be able to pray for our enemies, and may even be able to do some good deeds for our enemies. But one aspect of meekness that often gets overlooked is that it initiates—it acts first.

How many times have you heard, "Well, she has hurt me deeply, and I am not going to see that woman again until she comes here and apologizes!" We encounter many variations on that theme, probably because it sounds so fair. Why shouldn't bullies apologize to those they have punched? Yet the Bible sees things very differently.

"For God so loved the world that he sent his one and only Son" (John

3:16). "While we were *still* sinners, Christ died for us" (Rom. 5:8). Our rebellious world did not ask Him for help. He began to save us even when none of us were listening.

We see this explained clearly when Jesus discusses the problem of murder by word of mouth. In the Sermon on the Mount He concludes, "Therefore, if you are offering your gift at the altar and there remember that your brother has something against you, leave your gift there in front of the altar. First go and be reconciled to your brother; then come and offer your gift" (Matt. 5:23, 24). Notice carefully what Jesus says. If you "remember that your brother has something against you . . . go and be reconciled with your brother." I may not have a problem with my brother, but even if I think that someone has a problem with me, I am to go and initiate the healing process.

We might seek to squirm out of this situation. I don't have a problem—the other person's the one with it. Fortunately, because God did not see it that way with us, we have a chance for our broken relationship with Him to be restored, and to have eternal life. In the same sense, we may be the only avenue that our aggressor may have to eternal life, but it requires that we take the lead and open up the way.

4. Meekness does not try to defend itself under injustice, but trusts the situation to the Father. Earlier we considered the idea that pride is the primary enemy of meekness. We generally acknowledged that such pride is the root of sin and an enemy that must be overcome. Pride, when called by that name, is an obvious enemy. However, pride often masquerades as justice. No one can fault a call for justice. Wrongs must be made right, shouldn't they? Injustice must be stopped. The problem is that if we turn to justice instead of meekness, other enemies, close relatives of pride, can creep into our hearts. They're called bitterness and unforgiveness.

I visited a woman who had been fired from her job some years before. It had been a painful affair for all sides, but especially for her. As we talked, her hurt and anger bubbled under the surface of our conversation. She demanded justice—that something be done to correct the errors that had been made. And yes, I think errors had been made. Injustice may have taken place.

After a while I asked her directly, "Have you forgiven the people who did this to you?"

Pausing for a moment, she answered a little more quietly, "I'm not sure."

I think what she actually meant was no.

Leaving her house, I felt extremely sad. I believe peace and contentment could have been hers, even in the middle of injustice, if only she had chosen meekness first. If we are not careful, bitterness and resentment will coexist with our demands for injustice to be overturned, and they will poison our souls to death.

By contrast David, who had faced injustice for many years, declares, "My salvation and my honor depend on God; he is my mighty rock, my refuge. Trust in him at all times, O people; pour out your hearts to him, for God is our refuge" (Ps. 62:7, 8). I remember reading part of that text again and again—"my salvation and my honor depend on God." My honor depends on God?

I realized that at the heart of my own struggles for justice was the belief that I was responsible for my honor. At times that I felt that my reputation was being tarnished, I concluded that it was up to me to restore "the truth." But David was saying something very different and slightly risky. He claims that God will be responsible for my reputation. When this finally sunk in, I felt relieved. I didn't have to fight my own battles anymore; but to have peace I would have to trust Him.

Peter uses the life of Jesus as a model for his readers: "When they hurled their insults at him, he did not retaliate; when he suffered, he made no threats. Instead, he entrusted himself to him who judges justly" (1 Peter 2:23). In the same way, we don't remain silent just because we can't think of anything to say. Jesus did not remain silent because of a loss for words. Rather, we remain silent because God is working on our behalf. He will vindicate us.

Injustice will increasingly surround us, even in the church. Ellen White highlights this very clearly, but also tells us not to be alarmed by it. "Now is our time of peril. Our only safety is in walking in the footsteps of Christ, and wearing His yoke. Troublous times are before us. In many instances, friends will become alienated. Without cause, men will become our enemies. The motives of the people of God will be misinterpreted, not only by the world, but by their own brethren. The Lord's servants will be put in hard places. A mountain will be made of a molehill to justify men in pursuing a selfish, unrighteous course. The work that men have done faithfully will be disparaged and underrated, because apparent prosperity did not attend their efforts. By misrepresentation, these men will be clothed in the dark vestments of dishonesty, because circumstances beyond their control made their work perplexing. They will be pointed to as men that cannot be trusted. And this will be done by the members of the church. God's servants must arm themselves with the mind of Christ. They must not expect to escape insult and misjudgment. They will be called enthusiasts and fanatics. But let them not become discouraged. . . . God's hand is on the wheel of His providence, guiding His work to the glory of His name" (*The Upward Look,* p. 177).

Being Squeezed for Meekness

We have considered four facets to illustrate meekness, but how do we become meek? As we have already noted, if we desire to learn meekness, then rather than creating an overnight miracle in our hearts through an act of the Holy Spirit, God may place us into a crucible of painful circumstances.

In his writings Oswald Chambers uses the phrase "to be made broken bread and poured-out wine." If we are to become useful as wine for God, we will at some point need to be crushed. The problem is that God rarely squeezes us with His own fingers.

Chambers explains that "God can never make us wine if we object to the fingers He uses to crush us with. If God would only use His own fingers, and make me broken bread and poured-out wine in a special way! But when He uses someone whom we dislike, or some set of circumstances to which we said we would never submit, and makes those the crushers, we object. We must never choose the scene of our own martyrdom. If ever we are going to be made into wine, we will have to be crushed; you cannot drink grapes. Grapes become wine only when they have been squeezed" (*My Utmost for His Highest,* reading for Sept. 30).

Ezekiel certainly got squeezed. God suddenly interrupted his day by announcing the imminent death of his wife. "The word of the Lord came to me: 'Son of man, with one blow I am about to take away from you the delight of your eyes. Yet do not lament or weep or shed any tears. Groan quietly; do not mourn for the dead. Keep your turban fastened and your sandals on your feet; do not cover the lower part of your face or eat the customary food of mourners'" (Eze. 24:15-17).

Would you have been tempted to protest? I can imagine that howls of "But that's totally unfair!" would erupt from many people's mouths. But all that we hear from Ezekiel is "So I spoke to the people in the morning, and in the evening my wife died. The next morning I did as I had been commanded" (verse 18).

Remember the dictionary definition—"enduring injury with patience and without resentment"? Ezekiel manages, somehow, to endure, though I cannot begin to imagine his inner thoughts.

To be squeezed without becoming bitter wine cannot happen unless we have total confidence in God's sovereignty over our affairs. We have to believe that He somehow is bringing about all things for good—even though our hearts are breaking.

Faith in the Sovereignty of God

To believe that the sovereignty of God enables us to endure injury with patience and without resentment means that we have to believe that God is sovereign over everything. However, at one time I was taught that God was in charge of the big things, but that He left the smaller details for me to work out. I was familiar with Jesus' assurance: "Are not two sparrows sold for a penny? Yet not one of them will fall to the ground apart from the will of your Father. And even the very hairs of your head are all numbered. So don't be afraid; you are worth more than many sparrows" (Matt. 10:29-31). Yet somehow I and many others took the passage metaphorically rather than literally.

The idea that I was responsible for the lesser aspects of life bothered me, because I had always believed that God was intimately involved in everything. It took me some time to be certain that what I had been taught was wrong. As the years have gone by, I have been continually amazed at how God has participated in the smallest details of my life.

I was reminded of God's complete sovereignty over my life one day while waiting for a flight to the Westman Islands, just off the southern coast of Iceland, where I was going to preach. I arrived at the airport early and wanted to spend my waiting time doing something worthwhile. *What shall I do, Father?* I thought to myself. Although I had meant it to be a rhetorical question, I felt strongly impressed to make a written list of everything that I was thankful for.

But the impression left me confused. Why should I make a written list when I could very easily just go through it all in my head? But, somewhat reluctantly, I pulled out a paper and pen and began to write:

"Thanks:

"1. For Your love, which holds me tight.

"2. For Your sovereignty, which holds all things in harmony, purposefully.

"3. For Your repeated, gracious assurances of Your presence and guidance.

"4. For Your peace in the midst of the storm.

"5. That one day I will see You face to face and realize that everything has been worth it."

When I arrived at the church, I immediately began to look for a rubbish bin. It had begun to dawn on me that if I had to make a written list, there might come a time that I was going to have to read it again. What made the thought worse was that if my list was about things for which I was thankful, I might find myself reading it at a time I would be actually feeling very unthankful. It was an ominous feeling.

But when I finally found the bin, I could not bring myself to throw my list away. I stood staring at it and finally put it back in my Bible. I had a sheaf of papers with me, and so I buried my list in the middle of it. I did not want to read it again. Returning home, I put the papers out of sight.

Three days later one of God's crucibles arrived, and I felt devastated. It was one of those terrible disappointments that comes right out of the blue and takes your breath away.

A couple days after that, someone asked me to take the Sabbath school lesson at one of the churches. Turning to the subject, I noticed that it was on prayer and disappointment. I rolled my eyes. It was ironic, but also the very last thing I wanted to teach about.

By Friday I realized that I had to prepare for the lesson. At first I couldn't find writing paper anywhere, but finally I noticed a few sheets lying in a corner. Picking up my pen, I took a sheet and turned it over to begin writing—and stared. There facing me was my list. If ever there was a time that I needed to be reminded of what God had been doing in my life and how grateful I was to Him, it was then.

When we find ourselves under pressure from people and circumstances, we struggle with the temptation to think that God does not know about our situation. But Scripture tells us otherwise. "Why do you say, O Jacob, and complain, O Israel, 'My way is hidden from the Lord; my cause is disregarded by my God'? Do you not know? Have you not heard? The Lord is the everlasting God, the Creator of the ends of the earth. He will not grow tired or weary, and his understanding no one can fathom. He gives strength to the weary and increases the power of the weak. Even youths grow tired and weary, and young men stumble and fall; but those who hope in the Lord will renew their strength. They will soar on wings like eagles; they will run and not grow weary, they will walk and not be faint" (Isa. 40:27-31).

A Clear Connection With Heaven

As we have noted, meekness is not easy, because it regularly grows in a crucible. But in the middle of the turmoil that crucibles bring, meekness has the potential to offer peace to our own souls, as well as grace and eternity to those who cause us pain. Through meekness we bring Christ and His salvation into the world.

As you consider the call to meekness, think about this: "The difficulties we have to encounter may be very much lessened by that meekness which hides itself in Christ. If we possess the humility of our Master, we shall rise above the slights, the rebuffs, the annoyances, to which we are daily exposed, and they will cease to cast a gloom over the spirit. The highest evidence of nobility in a Christian is self-control. He who under abuse or cruelty fails to maintain a calm and trustful spirit robs God of His right to reveal in him His own perfection of character. Lowliness of heart is the strength that gives victory to the followers of Christ; it is the token of their connection with the courts above" (*The Desire of Ages,* p. 301).

> *Father,*
>> *Grant me the meekness of Jesus.*
>> *When I am insulted,*
>> *Or opposed,*
>> *Or crushed in circumstances I cannot control,*
>> *May I remain silent, and allow You to be the judge.*
>> *Take away my desire for revenge, even when I feel justified about it.*
>> *But replace it with love, love shown through my actions and intercession for the highest good of those who oppose me.*
> *In Jesus' name, amen.*

CHAPTER 11

Patience—
Faith in the Timing of God

"But the fruit of the Spirit is...patience..."
Galatians 5:22

Time magazine reported on an entertaining experiment with 4-year-olds and marshmallows. The researchers invited each 4-year-old into a plain room and told them that they could have a marshmallow. However, if the child waited until the scientist returned from an errand, they would receive two. The scientist then left the room.

The children then fell into two groups. One grabbed the marshmallow the moment the researcher left the room. The other group did everything they could to wait. They covered their eyes, sang to themselves, or amused themselves by playing games—anything to avoid being seduced by the marshmallow. When the scientist returned, the latter children received their promised reward.

The researchers then waited for the children to grow up. By the time the young people entered high school, a survey of their parents and teachers found that those children who had waited for the second marshmallow were generally "better adjusted, more popular, adventurous, confident and dependable teenagers. The children who gave in to temptation early on were more likely to be lonely, easily frustrated and stubborn. They buckled under stress and shied away from challenges. And when some of the students took the Scholastic Aptitude Test, the kids who had held out longer scored an average of 210 points higher" (Nancy Gibbs, "The EQ Factor," *Time,* Oct. 2, 1995).

The magazine article reports that when we consider brilliance we automatically think of people who are "wired for greatness from birth" and that greatness is somehow built into our IQ. But, the article reports, "it seems that the ability to delay gratification is a master skill, a triumph of the reasoning brain over the impulsive one." This is considered to be one important aspect of what has come to be called "emotional intelligence" (*ibid.*).

Time goes on to report on a book by Daniel Goleman, a Harvard psychology Ph.D. and New York *Times* science writer. Goleman's book, *Emotional Intelligence*, suggests that "when it comes to predicting people's success, brainpower as measured by IQ and standardized achievement tests may actually matter less than the qualities of mind once thought of as 'character' before the word began to sound quaint" (*ibid.*).

That's quite a conclusion. The researchers consider patience, the ability to wait for something without rushing to do what we feel like doing in the moment, "a master skill," and they regard such skills as more important than IQ to success.

The priority of patience was of course highlighted a long time before Goleman's book. "But the fruit of the Spirit is . . . patience" (Gal. 5:22). Patience is evidently high on God's agenda for us if we want to become more like Him.

What Patience Does

But what is patience and why is it necessary? Patience is simply the ability to wait calmly between the point at which we think something should be done and the point that God's will desires it to be done. Godly patience, therefore, is faith in God's timing.

Living according to His timing is important. However, there often exists a gap in time between when I am ready and when God is ready, and it can make us frustrated. Learning to wait patiently during this period enables us to remain within God's will, and the waiting time itself can contribute to our spiritual maturity. Consider the following spiritual purposes of waiting.

1. Waiting refocuses our minds away from things and back to God Himself. We can be so obsessed with things—even good things from God—that He needs to redirect our thoughts back to Him. It's the giver of the things, not the things themselves, that is important.

When David encourages us not to let the success of the wicked overwhelm us, he writes, "Be still before the Lord and wait patiently for him" (Ps. 37:7). I am not exactly sure what David was thinking when he wrote this, but it appears he wants us to look at the person of God. It's not simply that the Lord will come and get revenge for us or that He will vindicate us. It is that the presence of God Himself is what really matters, for what can anyone do when He is with us? However, sometimes it takes time for this truth to sink in. So the Lord may permit a crucible experience in which we learn how to wait patiently while refocusing our thoughts on Him.

2. Waiting allows us to have a clearer picture of ourselves. Sometimes we understand our own motives only after time has gone by. Thus waiting becomes an opportunity to examine ourselves. Occasionally we are absolutely certain of what we want and are desperate for it. But it is only as time passes that we begin to realize that what we once thought was the most desirable thing in the world actually isn't. I wonder how much heartache we could avoid if we had more time to assess ourselves before we act.

3. Waiting builds spiritual stamina. In Western cultures particularly, we have become almost obsessed with the instant. We have instant photos and instant food and instant everything else. I even saw an advertisement in the window of a real estate agency promising me that I could buy a house within 30 minutes. Getting what we want immediately can be a real problem. Our tempers easily flare the moment someone pauses at a green light, or an elderly person fumbles around in their purse at the supermarket checkout.

Consider the classic example of a student wanting to know if she could finish her college course more quickly by taking shorter classes. The teacher said that it was possible, but that it all depended on what she wanted to become.

It is the same when God grows us spiritually. We could bloom to maturity within months and gain the strength of a pumpkin. Or we could wait patiently for the years to go by and develop the strength of an oak tree. Which would you rather be?

4. Waiting develops other spiritual strengths, such as faith and trust. Waiting is a key that opens the door to understanding many spiritual things. James writes about this in a way that often seems hard to grasp: "Consider it pure joy, my brothers, whenever you face trials of many kinds, because you know that the testing of your faith develops perseverance. Perseverance must finish its work so that you may be mature and complete, not lacking anything" (James 1:2-4). So waiting develops God's other graces in us more fully.

5. Waiting allows God to implement other pieces of His plan that He needs to complete first. "But when the time had fully come, God sent his Son" (Gal. 4:4). God did not send Jesus immediately after Adam and Eve sinned. Humanity had to wait before He came. God had other things to do in the meantime. Before He deals with the issue that burns in our minds right now, there may be some other things He needs to finish before He comes to the part about which we are most concerned.

6. Waiting may be to test us. If we don't get an immediate response from God, we may find ourselves turning away and looking somewhere else. The Lord sometimes allows us to wait in order to test us—to see if we will really cling to what He has said.

Such was the experience of Abraham. God permitted 25 years to lapse between the original promise of Abraham becoming the father of a nation and the arrival of Isaac. Unfortunately, the patriarch couldn't wait. About 15 years before the arrival of Isaac, he slept with his wife's servant Hagar. It is vital to realize that such times of delay and "experiences that test faith are for our benefit. . . . Faith is strengthened by exercise. We must let patience have its perfect work, remembering that there are precious promises in the Scriptures for those who wait upon the Lord" (Ellen G. White, *Gospel Workers*, p. 219).

7. Waiting may be for . . . ? We may never know the reason. Over a period of months, many times Ellen White could only sleep for just a couple hours a night. She noted, "I cannot read the purpose of God in my affliction, but He knows what is best, and I will commit my soul, body, and spirit to Him as unto my faithful Creator" (*Selected Messages,* book 2, p. 242).

We may encounter delays that we will never understand this side of heaven. But this should not cause us concern. As Ellen White continued: "If we educated and trained our souls to have more faith, more love, greater patience, and a more perfect trust in our heavenly Father, I know we would have more peace and happiness day by day as we pass through the conflicts of this life.

"The Lord is not pleased to have us fret and worry ourselves out of the arms of Jesus. More is needed of the quiet waiting and watching combined. We think unless we have feeling that we are not in the right track, and we keep looking within for some sign befitting the occasion; but the reckoning is not of feeling but of faith" (*ibid.*).

All in God's Time

While we can learn many things from waiting, it's not something easy—at least for me. I remember when I moved to Iceland and needed to buy a car. A friend and I drove to an auto dealer, and suddenly we saw just what I was looking for. It was a 2-year-old Toyota Corolla, a beautiful midnight blue. I had been driving an elderly VW Golf that I had just given to my brother, and this Toyota was not just a step up—it was in a different league altogether.

The dealer promised a 20 percent discount, and so we took it for a test drive. Compared to my Golf, it drove like a dream. It also had a CD player—no more scratchy cassette tapes.

Returning to the dealer, I put in an offer just below the asking price. Even if the dealership did not accept it, I still had enough money to pay the full amount.

The dealer was selling the car on behalf of a private individual, so he had to call him and get back to me. In the meantime I decided to go back to the car to check its stereo system. The sound was amazing. I had never heard such clarity in a car before. Happily I returned to the office, where the salesman stunned me with his next words. "I'm sorry," he said awkwardly. "Someone else has just bought the car."

As I had been sitting in the car listening to a CD, another person, who had seen the car earlier in the day, had walked into the sales office and handed another salesman the full cash amount. I was speechless.

How could God let this happen to me after all the prayers I had prayed? He knew I needed a car, and this was the only one that had such a large discount. Feeling that my answer to prayer had been stolen from me, I was—to put it mildly—annoyed.

For a couple days I felt very confused and let down. I had prayed hard about a car; then I had seen the very vehicle I knew I needed, and yet it was swiped away from under my nose. God was unfair.

Three days later my friend and I looked at the cars at the main Toyota dealership. Normally such dealers are much more expensive than the independent ones. As we drove around, I spotted it—an identical 2-year-old midnight-blue Corolla. As I looked through the window I saw on the dash a CD player. It was virtually the same car—except that it had fewer kilometers on the odometer and, to my surprise, was even US$100 cheaper.

I learned something important that day. Good things come from God, but they come in His timing—not when my heart decides to own them.

Faith in God's Timing

The story of David's patience in becoming king is a fascinating example of one young man who resolved not to grab divine promises before the right time.

After Saul began drifting from God, 1 Samuel begins to describe how the Lord sent the prophet Samuel to anoint a new king. God directed him to Jesse's house and pointed out the teenage David as the chosen one.

Can you imagine how David must have felt? A young teenager being anointed to the most powerful position under God, called to be king over His people?

If that had happened to me, I would not have slept much that night! My mind would have whirled with all sorts of ideas, strategies, plans, dreams— what a future was in store! What wealth, what privilege, what responsibility to lead and to rule. Night after night I would have been dreaming about what I was going to do. Perhaps I would have even begun to expect a little more respect from my brothers. So when was it all going to happen?

But David went back to looking after his sheep.

Some time later while he cared for the flock, a messenger arrived at David's home and asked if he would go to the palace to play his harp for the king. Saul struggled with depression and had heard from one of his advisors that David could play a soothing tune. You can imagine David thinking, *Is this the beginning of the road to the throne?* Within a short period of time King Saul made David one of his armor bearers.

Things moved at quite a pace. David dramatically killed Goliath, distinguished himself in battle, and received a high rank in the army. The young man did well, and all the people sang his praises. His friendship with Jonathan grew, but during this time Saul became jealous of David's success and began to hunt him down to kill him. But both Jonathan and Saul knew what was going to happen. "'Don't be afraid,' he [told David]. 'My father Saul will not lay a hand on you. You will be king over Israel, and I will be second to you. Even my father Saul knows this'" (1 Sam. 23:17).

Here is the interesting point. David knew that he was going to be king. Jonathan recognized that David would become the next ruler. Even Saul later admitted to David that he would gain the throne. But David never did anything to promote himself as king.

In fact, he seemed to run in the opposite direction. Another day as Saul sought to track him down again, the king accidentally went into a cave where David and his men had hidden. What a wonderful opportunity for David to kill the man who had been hunting him. God's promises could now be fulfilled. However, instead of slaying his persecutor, David snipped off a tiny piece of Saul's robe. But "afterward, David was conscience-stricken for having cut off a corner of his robe. He said to his men, 'The Lord forbid that I should do such a thing to my master, the Lord's anointed, or lift my hand against him; for he is the anointed of the Lord.' With these words David rebuked his men and did not allow them to attack Saul. And Saul left the cave and went his way" (1 Sam. 24:5-7).

Imagine: Saul was trying to kill David. David had a very good opportunity to stop his enemy, but was now feeling terrible for even taking a little piece of his robe!

And it happened again. Saul was out on another expedition to kill David. David and Abishai sneaked up on the sleeping king, and Abishai suggested, "'Today God has delivered your enemy into your hands. Now let me pin him to the ground with one thrust of my spear; I won't strike him twice.' But David said to Abishai, 'Don't destroy him! Who can lay a hand on the Lord's anointed and be guiltless? As surely as the Lord lives,' he said, 'the Lord himself will strike him; either his time will come and he will die, or he will go into battle and perish. But the Lord forbid that I should lay a hand on the Lord's anointed'" (1 Sam. 26:8-11).

I wonder how many of us would have felt justified in grabbing Saul's crown?

The message of David's life is clear. God's promises are best enjoyed when received from His own hands, in His own way, and in His own timing.

The Problem of Rushing

When we rush ahead of God's timing, we miss out on the perfection of His will for us. Especially when we are in the crucible we find a number of emotions bubble up within our hearts that threaten to push us outside of God purposes.

Consider how the following people lost out because of such impatience:

Jonah: God's will missed because of a wounded and impatient ego. Poor Jonah. God's messenger of grace and mercy had finally preached His words to the people of Nineveh, and unfortunately a revival had broken out. "But Jonah was greatly displeased and became angry. He prayed to the Lord, 'O Lord, is this not what I said when I was still at home? That is why I was so quick to flee to Tarshish. I knew that you are a gracious and compassionate God, slow to anger and abounding in love, a God who relents from sending calamity. Now, O Lord, take away my life, for it is better for me to die than to live" (Jonah 4:1-3).

He is angry at God's forgiveness because he thought it made him look like a false prophet. Later Jonah gets mad at God again after the vine He gave him for shade in the blistering heat gets withered by a worm. "But God said to Jonah, 'Do you have a right to be angry about the vine?' 'I do,' he said. 'I am angry enough to die'" (verse 9).

Strong words from a prophet to his Creator! Jonah's ego was so wounded that it rushed him past the possibility of him becoming a show-case for God's grace. Instead he launched one of the most famous pity parties of all time and became infamous throughout history.

Elijah: God's will missed by an impatience driven by fear. After the big showdown on Mount Carmel, Elijah ran through the blinding rain in order to guide King Ahab back to his palace. As soon as Ahab got inside, he rushed to find his wife. "Now Ahab told Jezebel everything Elijah had done and how he had killed all the prophets with the sword. So Jezebel sent a messenger to Elijah to say, 'May the gods deal with me, be it ever so severely, if by this time tomorrow I do not make your life like that of one of them'" (1 Kings 19:1, 2).

How did Elijah respond? "Elijah was afraid and ran for his life" (verse 3). Off he fled into the desert. His fear driving him, he raced into despair. Then "he came to a broom tree, sat down under it and prayed that he might die. 'I have had enough, Lord,' he said. 'Take my life'" (verse 4).

As God tried to rehabilitate His weary prophet, the question came to Elijah twice: "What are you doing here, Elijah?" (verse 9). Elijah was in the wrong place. His fear had driven him away from where God wanted him to be, and the consequences were enormous. "Had he remained where he was, had he made God his refuge and strength, standing steadfast for the truth, he would have been shielded from harm. The Lord would have given him another signal victory by sending His judgements on Jezebel; and the impression made on the king and the people would have wrought a great reformation" (Ellen G. White, *Prophets and Kings* [Mountain View, Calif.: Pacific Press Pub. Assn., 1917], p. 160).

Judas and Peter: God's will missed by impatient ambition. Judas is perhaps an unavoidable example of God's will missed by ambition. He had plans for Jesus, but he rushed on with them before he allowed time for Jesus' teaching to sink in.

But Judas was not the only one. Peter had other ideas too. "[Jesus] then began to teach them that the Son of Man must suffer many things and be rejected by the elders, chief priests and teachers of the law, and that he must be killed and after three days rise again. He spoke plainly about this, and Peter took him aside and began to rebuke him" (Mark 8:31, 32). The word Mark uses for Peter's rebuking of Jesus is the same word that he employed to describe Jesus casting out the evil spirits in Mark 1. Peter is talking tough, but his mouth is racing faster than his brain can understand the purposes of God. Again, in Gethsemane, Peter's sword works faster than his brain as he lashes out at those who come to take Jesus. The disciple had ambitions also, but unlike Judas, the crucible caused him to pause and re-consider his direction.

Adam: God's will missed by impatient love. I knew of a young man in tears because he was sleeping with the woman he loved, but they were not married, and he knew from the Bible that it wasn't right. He decided to pray and ask God what to do, but received no answer. So since they did not get what he thought should be a divine response, they continued living together.

God's answer was clearly written in the Bible, but his love for the woman had caused him to demand more.

It was very similar with Adam. When Eve came to him with the fruit in her hand, God's will for Adam was still quite clear. "You must not eat from the tree of the knowledge of good and evil, for when you eat of it you will surely die" (Gen. 2:17). Adam was not deceived by a snake, as Eve had been. He made a conscious choice to join her in her fate, and so took the fruit and ate it. "His love for Eve was strong, and in utter discouragement he resolved to share her fate. He seized the fruit and quickly ate it. . . . Adam, through his love for Eve, disobeyed the command of God, and fell with her" (Ellen G. White, *Early Writings*, p. 148). His deep longing for Eve quickly took him outside of God's will.

Such impatient love is causing great tragedy in our world. So Solomon's advice is wise: "Do not arouse or awaken love until it so desires" (Song of Sol. 2:7; 3:5; 8:4).

Grace When We Mess Up

Wounded egos, fear, ambition, love—many things threaten to derail God's will for us, but the principle is always the same. Strong emotion can be so blinding that we miss what is truly important. But what happens when we mess up and find ourselves having rushed outside of God's will?

In a Hebrew class at college I learned about a memorable Hebrew expression Scripture uses to describe God's long-suffering and patience. The phrase used literally means "an extension of the nostrils." The idea is that when someone gets angry, they get red in the face and their nose flares. You may have seen this sometimes! However, if the nose is very long, it will take more time for the whole nose to become red. So in this sense God has a long nose. It takes a very long time before He becomes impatient with us.

God's grace for the impatient is never far away. His response to Elijah is a good example of His dealings with His impatient followers. "Did God forsake Elijah in his hour of trial? Oh, no! He loved His servant no less when Elijah felt himself forsaken of God and man than when, in answer to his prayer, fire flashed from heaven and illuminated the mountain top. And now, as Elijah slept, a soft touch and a pleasant voice awoke him. He started up in terror, as if to flee, fearing that the enemy had discovered him. But the pitying face bending over him was not the face of an enemy, but of a friend" (Ellen G. White, *Prophets and Kings,* p. 166).

Don't Try to Shortcut the Waiting Time

When we get frustrated while waiting in the crucible, it can be so tempting to jump ahead and do something ourselves to relieve the pressure. But it is very dangerous to escape the waiting time too early, because we may be running ahead of God. It is only by waiting on Him that we will experience the full beauty of His purposes. As Solomon wrote: "He has made everything beautiful in its time" (Eccl. 3:11).

I received a forwarded e-mail that had obviously traveled a lot around the Internet, but it illustrated an important truth about waiting for God's perfect time. A young pastor came to meet his mentor for some advice on God's will for his life. As they were walking in the garden, the younger man asked what he should do. The older pastor picked a rosebud from a nearby bush and handed it to him. "Please open the bud," he asked, "but don't tear any of the petals." The young pastor was not sure what to do, and wondered what the rose had to do with knowing the will of God. It looked like an impossible task, and as he tried to peel back the petals, he found that it was. At this point his mentor began to recite a poem by Charlie Gilchrist that compared that relatively simple task to complexity of managing one's life, and emphasized the wisdom of leaving both in the hands of God.

While we wait, we may be tempted to doubt everything. But it is at such times that we need to rouse our wills and place our dreams back in the hands of our Father, and abandon ourselves to His care.

"Wait on the Lord; be of good courage, and He shall strengthen your heart; wait, I say, on the Lord!" (Ps. 27:14, NKJV).

Father,
   Teach me patience, for it keeps me close to You.
   Teach me to understand the perfection of Your timing;
   To rest peacefully in the knowledge that all things in my life are under Your
      loving care.
   And that even Your pauses have meaning and purpose.
In Jesus' name, amen.

CHAPTER 12

Submission—
Faith in the Will of God

"I tell you the truth, unless a kernel of wheat falls to the
ground and dies, it remains only a single seed.
But if it dies, it produces many seeds."
John 12:24

The word "submission" sends shivers down many people's backs. Yet the Bible—even in the new versions—uses the word quite often. Hezekiah called on God's people to "submit to the Lord" (2 Chron. 30:8). God bemoans the fact that his people "would not submit to me" (Ps. 81:11). Paul regrets that the natural mind "does not submit to God's law" (Rom. 8:7). The apostle also uses the church as a model for our lives because it "submits to Christ" (Eph. 5:24). And James calls on us all to "submit yourselves, then, to God" (James 4:7).

In our world the word "submit" sounds harsh and unjust, but that is not meant to be part of the biblical understanding. Such submission is to the person of God, and concerns abandoning our fallen humanity for His holiness and giving up our own dreams for His infinite plans. Amy Carmichael suggests that another word to help us understand submission is "acceptance"—of our Father's will (Amy Carmichael, *Learning of God*, p. 53).

Because of the bad connotations that submission has within our culture, we have struggled to apply its meaning and importance to our lives. As a result, I think we have failed to grasp what is at the heart of discipleship—the call to our own crucifixion. But all true biblical discipleship begins with death, a death to which we must willingly submit.

Learning to Submit Is Not a Pleasant Journey

My own journey in understanding this has not been easy or enjoyable. At the beginning of my ministry I came across the classic devotional *My Utmost for His Highest*, by Oswald Chambers. Chambers tirelessly puts forward the case that if we are to become useful for God's kingdom we must abandon to Him everything we have and everything we are. "No one enters into the experience of entire sanctification without going through a 'white funeral'—the burial of the old life. If there has never been this crisis of death, sanctification is nothing more than a vision. Have you come to your last days really? You have come to them often in sentiment, but have you come to them *really?* . . . We skirt the cemetery and all the time refuse to go to death. Have you had your 'white funeral,' or are you sacredly playing the fool with your soul? Is there a place in your life marked as the last day, a place to which the memory goes back with a chastened and extraordinary grateful remembrance, 'Yes, it was then, at that "white funeral" that I made an agreement with God' " (*My Utmost for His Highest,* reading for Jan. 15).

I decided that I needed to learn what this meant, so opening my journal, I wrote, "Father, I would really like to know what this abandonment is all about." It seemed that no sooner had the prayer rushed past my lips than everything in my life began to disintegrate.

The first thing to go was my health. A short time after my abandonment prayer I toured West Africa with some friends. Flying back from Togo to the Ivory Coast on the last leg of my trip, I began to feel a little cold. The next morning, as I caught my plane to Zurich, I started shaking.

On returning to England, I was put immediately into isolation because the physicians thought I had a contagious disease and was bleeding internally. The doctors eventually concluded that I had an "unknown African virus," which simply meant that you feel very sick and no one really knows why. This was not good, because the patient's dining room had a list on which you could write your name and your disease. The more deadly the disease you had, the more points you got. On a scale of one to 10, 10 being the highest, the "unknown African virus" got one point. You could get bonus points if you arrived at the hospital by air ambulance, but minus points if your mother drove you. I started with a negative score!

I left the hospital after five days, but relapsed and had to return immediately, where I encountered more needles. By now I had no energy. Even talking to my family on the phone was exhausting. It was four months before I regained enough strength to begin work, but even then, I knew that I was not as strong as I once was. I felt something had broken inside.

The next thing I lost was my reputation. As I mentioned in an earlier chapter, after a couple days in the hospital I received a letter tearing apart the work that I thought I had been doing well, and it seemed as if the whole world had received copies of it. I was bewildered and deeply hurt, and because of my physical illness I could do little to defend myself.

Then the gossip started. Every morning I would wake up thinking about what I had heard along the grapevine regarding the letter. I couldn't stop the thoughts from racing round and round in my head, hour after hour.

Next it was my job. As I was sick, my first-year contract did not get renewed. To my surprise, someone at the office even insinuated that the renewal was not necessary, as I might not ever be well enough to work again.

Then it was back to my health. During some tests at the tropical diseases hospital the doctors found that I had a problem with my heart. The physicians decided that I, even though only 27, needed a pacemaker. I had been extremely tired for a number of years, which was embarrassing. I would arrive at someone's house for a Bible study and had difficulty making conversation, as it was hard for me to think clearly.

The pacemaker operation was a memorable experience. Everything that could go wrong did. Halfway through the operation I heard the surgeon announce, "He's got some tough tissue here. I'm not sure what to do." The surgeon called to get help from a specialist, but after no answer he left the room to find assistance.

Finally returning, he said cheerfully to the nurses, "I can't find the specialist—I'll have to have a go myself." Pacemaker operations use only a local anaesthetic, so I was fully conscious and not brimming with confidence at what I heard. Then as the operation had gone on longer than expected, the anaesthetic began to wear off.

"Can I have some more anaesthetic, please?" I asked.

"I'm sorry," the nurse said compassionately, "but you have had all we are allowed to give you."

Perhaps as an afterthought, because of all their banging around on my chest, the surgeon had managed to puncture my pleural sac, which collapsed one lung. The next day a group of medical students gathered around my bed to see if they could figure out what was wrong with me. None of them guessed correctly. Then they put a big syringe in my back between my ribs, and sucked out almost a liter of air from around my lungs.

Five days after I left the hospital the area around the pacemaker got infected. When I went for a checkup, the nurse's eyes quickly widened as she murmured under her breath, "Oh, no." The surgical team who were packing up for the weekend immediately unpacked, and demanded that I go into the operating room immediately. Removing the pacemaker, they scrubbed me hard with disinfectant and then sewed everything back up.

A month later I was back for the procedure to start all over again.

Finally it was my personal life. Two weeks after the insertion of the second pacemaker my girlfriend and I ended our several-year-long relationship. I realize that that often happens to many people, but for me right then it was the last straw.

During a 12-month period I had lost my health, my job, my reputation, and my dreams of future happiness. I felt like Job, with someone systematically going through my life and knocking away everything that I was and everything that I had to depend on. Every area of my life seemed to be in pieces. I felt a profound sense of emptiness and exhaustion.

"God," I murmured, "the Bible says that the Holy Spirit prays for us. Will He please pray for me right now, because I haven't a clue what to say."

I wasn't waiting for an answer, but within seconds a peace that I could not explain came into my heart, and a smile began to creep rather unexpectedly across my face. A sense of deep contentment filled me. I felt as though God was standing right next to me.

That night I went to sleep smiling. I don't find it very easy to smile and sleep at the same time, but smiling I was. During the night I remember waking very briefly, and I was still smiling. Then I woke up in the morning with a smile still stuck all over my face.

As I lay in bed, all my fingers and toes were tingling. It is hard to describe it any other way, but it was as if jets of energy were pulsating around my body. I still didn't think anything until I walked into town. As I went along I realized that for the first time in years I was rushing.

My friends had always made jokes about me in the past. I was always in a hurry, which meant that my head always seemed to arrive before my feet. I walked as though I was leaning into some imaginary wind. And it was happening again. The family couch potato had suddenly transformed into a live wire, bouncing around somewhat unpredictably, and everyone was struggling to keep up. The change, over one night, was miraculous.

My energy was not the only thing to increase. I had also developed an urge to pray in a way that I had never experienced in my life. Every day I wanted to talk to God longer and longer.

But some weeks later it turned ugly, as I began to feel sorry for myself. I knew that after all that God had done for me, my attitude was wrong—indeed, I believed it was sinful, because I was complaining directly against His goodness. From that day, little by little, my energy began to disappear.

Then I got angry. "How can You do this?" I cried to God. "You have taken away everything from me, and now You are removing my health again, the only thing I have to rely on. It is not fair!" My daily spiritual battle with God was so intense that I would be physically exhausted by the time I got to bed.

This battle raged for two months. Finally one day I cried out loud, "Look, You have taken away everything from me—my health, my reputation. You took my job and my dreams. I have nothing!"

The voice of the Holy Spirit was unmistakable. "Yes, that is the point. I want you with nothing."

I was stunned. God wanted me with nothing?

Absolutely.

We come to God with so much we want to offer Him, but our humanness often gets in the way. So our Father frequently uses crucibles to help relieve us of the things that have consciously or unconsciously caused us to depend upon ourselves rather than completely upon him. As Charles Swindoll observes: "Being stripped of all substitutes is the most painful experience on earth" (Charles Swindoll, *David: Great Lives From God's Word* [Nashville: Word Pub. Co., 1997], p. 70).

One time I spoke to a student starting his ministerial training. I am always curious as to why people choose to become pastors, as often an interesting story lies behind the decision.

"So what made you decide to train for the ministry?" I asked.

"Well," the young student replied, "I think I have a lot to offer."

I was so amazed that I couldn't say anything. I wanted to shout, "Who cares what you have to offer! People need to hear about what God has to offer!" Fortunately, my mouth remained shut. But the truth is that God wants us with nothing, so that He can be everything.

Dying Like a Seed

The process of becoming nothing before God is the process of dying. Jesus describes it as dying like a seed. "I tell you the truth, unless a kernel of wheat falls to the ground and dies, it remains only a single seed. But if it dies, it produces many seeds" (John 12:24). While Jesus here refers to Himself as a seed dying, He summons His followers to the same death. "If anyone would come after me, he must deny himself and take up his cross and follow me" (Mark 8:34). Such following is not just wandering with a heavy burden along what many call "the Christian path." When Jesus spoke these words, He was on His way to Jerusalem—and to death. All those who would follow Him must do the same. They must follow Him to death.

Picking up the imagery from these verses, Elisabeth Elliot expands on this process of dying like a seed.

"The growth of all living green things wonderfully represents the process of receiving and relinquishing, gaining and losing, living and dying. The seed falls into the ground, dies as the new shoot springs up. There must be a splitting and a breaking in order for a bud to form. The calyx lets go of the flower. The petals must curl up and die in order for the fruit to form. The fruit falls, splits, relinquishes the seed. The seed falls to the ground. . . . There is no ongoing spiritual life without this process of letting go. At the precise point where we refuse, growth stops. If we hold tightly to anything given to us, unwilling to let it go when the time comes to let it go or unwilling to allow it to be used as the Giver means it to be used, we stunt the growth of the soul. . . . The seed does not 'know' what will happen. It only knows what is happening—the falling, the darkness, the dying. . . . God's ultimate plan [is] as far beyond our imaginings as the oak tree is from the acorn's imaginings. . . . The acorn does what it is meant to do, without pestering its Maker with questions about when and how and why. We who have been given an intelligence and a will and a whole range of wants that can be set against the divine Pattern for Good are asked to believe Him" (Elisabeth Elliot, *Passion and Purity* [Grand Rapids: Fleming H. Revell, 1984], pp. 162-165).

Let me highlight three parts of this submission process:

1. When the seed is dying, it does not know anything, especially what the future will hold. There will always be times that answers cannot be known today. This may lead to periods of darkness and confusion, for we reason that God seems uninterested in our situation. We also clamor for Him to reveal the future, but again we encounter only silence. The reality is that a seed is not yet a tree or a flower, so it cannot begin to imagine what such a new life will be like. Throughout this process we don't need to worry that God is not concerned. He is with us in the darkness, and He knows exactly what our new lives will bring.

2. Resurrection and fruitfulness happens only after death. Although it is an obvious truth, we still struggle to grasp it when it involves us. Transformation needs death to occur first. If you long for transformation, what is old and ugly and sinful must first be removed, and death is the only way for it to happen.

3. When God takes us to the point of dying like a seed, it is a call to trust. The death of the seed is not purposeless just because the seed falls to the ground and does not suddenly become a blossoming flower or majestic oak. The falling away, the darkness, and the waiting is essential to the preparation of the new life. Before that moment of new life breaks upon us, the quiet time of unknowing is a necessary time, handed to us from our loving Father to mature our trust in Him.

How will God bring you to this point of total surrender? It's hard to predict, but you will certainly know it when it happens. The point of total submission often comes only when we are in the center of the crucible, because the crucible is normally the only place that God can remove the selfish hankering of our hearts. No person learns to truly offer themselves to Jesus unreservedly unless they are at their wits' end (Oswald Chambers, *My Utmost for His Highest*, reading for Aug. 28). At that moment, when we are willing to offer God everything, we yield up what we have hung on to the longest, and He takes control. I think this is what the disciples started to understand as they began to wait together before Pentecost.

Elisabeth Elliot makes a profound claim about the high purpose of submission. "The surrender of our heart's deepest longing is perhaps as close as we come to an understanding of the cross. . . . Our own experience of crucifixion, though immeasurably less than our Saviour's, nonetheless furnishes us with a chance to begin to know Him in the fellowship of His suffering. In every form of our own suffering, He calls us into that fellowship" (*Quest for Love*, p. 182). She does not make her claim lightly. Elliot was one of the young wives whose missionary husbands were murdered by Indians in the jungles of Ecuador in 1956. Yet even such terrible tragedies, she suggests, can become paths into a deeper intimacy with God than we could have ever experienced before.

Adolph Monod emphasises how such deep crucibles can also bring the greatest joy and purpose. "And if among the trials that you are called to bear, there is one that seems, I do not say heavier than the others, but more compromising to your ministry, and likely to ruin forever the hopes of your holy mission, if outward temptations be added to these coming from within, if all seems assailed, body, mind, spirit, if all seems lost without remedy, well, accept this trial, shall I say, or this assemblage of trials, in a peculiar feeling of submission, hope and gratitude, as a trial in which the Lord will cause you to find a new mission. Hail it as the beginning of a ministry of weakness and bitterness . . . which He will cause to abound in more living fruit than your ministry of strength and joy in days gone by ever yielded" (in Amy Carmichael, *Learning of God*, p. 52).

Jesus—Our Model in Submission

Could Monod possibly be right? Could a ministry of weakness and tears be a reason for joy and a doorway into increasing fruitfulness?

Jesus' submission to His Father's will, though under great trial, seems to give us a resounding yes. Paul outlines three main parts of Jesus' descent into such a painful yet fruitful ministry.

The apostle advises, "Your attitude should be the same as that of Christ Jesus: who, being in very nature God, did not consider equality with God something to be grasped, but made himself nothing, taking the very nature of a servant, being made in human likeness. And being found in appearance as a man, he humbled himself and became obedient to death—even death on a cross!" (Phil. 2:5-8).

Notice three steps involved in the process of His submitting fully to the Father's will.

1. Jesus gave up His rights to equality. He was "in very nature God," but if He had not given up His right to stay in heaven in continual glory, He would not have succeeded in rescuing us. Likewise, if we are not prepared to give up what we consider to be "our rights," we may find the door to the reconciliation of broken relationships and service blocked.

2. Jesus gave up His rights to being a free citizen. He did not come with even the freedoms of an ordinary man. He arrived in "the very nature of a servant." The same is also true for us. As Peter, Paul, James, and Jude begin their letters in the New Testament, they proudly identify themselves as servants of God and of Jesus Christ. Servanthood is fundamental to the Christian's existence.

3. Jesus gave up His rights to life. He could not have accomplished His mission had He remained alive. It required his death, "even death on a cross!"

This downward three-step process emphasizes service as the primary goal of submission. Christian submission, which is always submission to God's will, is always to enable our Father to work freely through us for the good of ourselves, for the good of others, and for the glory of His name.

Chambers again fearlessly describes how God works in this process. "Our permission is never asked as to what we will do or where we will go. God makes us broken bread and poured-out wine to please Himself. To be 'separated unto the gospel' means to hear the call of God; and when a man begins to overhear that call, then begins agony that is worthy of the name. Every ambition is nipped in the bud, every desire of life quenched, every outlook completely extinguished and blotted out, saving one thing only—'*separated unto the gospel.*' Woe be to the soul who tries to put his foot in any other direction when once the call has come to him" (*My Utmost for His Highest,* reading for Feb. 2).

Gambling on Death

This process of dying is a holy gamble. Jesus calls us to risk everything without any specific guarantees as to the outcome, except the general promise that He will give us abundant life. But because we are scared of gambling our ambitions and dreams without God's providing a clear career path in advance, we are generally reticent to play.

While working in Albania, I took some visitors around the country. As the car bumped along the road, we began discussing the future. Someone then asked me, "So what are your plans for the future?"

I told the group that I didn't have any plans. I was going to concentrate on what God had given me to do today, and allow Him to shape what would come later.

Obviously they did not consider it a good answer, as they spent the next several minutes trying to correct my foolishness.

I'm sure they meant well, but I still have to disagree with their perspective. Sure, we can't blindly plow through life without thought or responsibility. But I have chosen to use my mind to submit to God's plans, and allow Him to become ultimately responsible for my life.

Perhaps you think that's a little naive or risky. But I think that Paul in the book of Romans calls for us to take that risk. "Therefore, I urge you, brothers, in view of God's mercy, to offer your bodies as living sacrifices, holy and pleasing to God—this is your spiritual act of worship" (Rom. 12:1). The apostle argues that the death of Christ that gives us salvation is a good enough reason to risk dying ourselves. But his argument has more to it than that. Paul claims that such a death determines whether we will be able to know God's will in the future.

"Do not conform any longer to the pattern of this world," the apostle continues, "but be transformed by the renewing of your mind. Then you will be able to test and approve what God's will is—his good, pleasing and perfect will" (verse 2). When you put these two texts together, I think we can see that knowing the will of God clearly comes after we have made our total sacrifice to Him. But then again, perhaps we won't see this very far in advance. Perhaps we will recognize it only one day at a time—for why else does Paul need to "die daily"? (1 Cor. 15:31, KJV)?

Practically, this sacrifice means that we commit without knowing what the future will hold. This "not knowing" can also mimic the experience of crucifixion. T. C. Upham describes its anguish: "The disposition ... to leave the dearest objects of our hearts in the sublime keeping of the general and unspecific belief that God is now answering our prayers in His own time and way, and in the best manner, involves a present process of inward crucifixion which is obviously unfavourable to the growth and even the existence of the life of self" (in Elisabeth Elliot, *Passion and Purity,* p. 150).

These days it is popular to hear all sorts of seminars and read a multitude of books that promise insights into knowing God's will for our lives. I can't help wondering if this is a symptom of our general reluctance to take Paul's advice. You see, when we die to Christ, knowing God's will for us quickly becomes irrelevant. For after death to ourselves, knowing the "what" of God's will suddenly becomes a lot less important than fellowship with the "who" of relationship with Him.

How Long Will It Take?

I received a phone call from a girl who sounded quite distressed.

"Hi, Maya. How are you?"

"Not good. Will you pray for me?"

"What's the problem?"

"Well, I'm doing things that I know I should not be doing, and God seems far away. How can I get back to where I am supposed to be?" She was quite emotional and obviously agitated as she spoke.

It was not a new conversation. We had gone through it a number of times before. I realized that I probably needed to become a little more blunt.

"Listen, Maya. We can pray and pray about this, but at the end of the day it will always come back to the same basic choice: Are you willing to offer yourself to God 100 percent, no strings attached? Can you honestly say to Him that you will go where He wants you to go, and do what He wants you to do—no matter how different it may be from what you have in mind right now? It's not about the big decisions you have coming up tomorrow. Rather, it's an attitude—an attitude toward God and life in general. If you want Him to work in your life, you have to give Him something to work with. Can you say that to Him?"

After a short pause, she replied, "I don't think I am ready for that just yet."

My heart grieved for her. I knew that until she fully submitted herself to her Father's will, she would keep falling and falling.

The Refiner's Fire

Are you ready to submit all that you are to your Father? If you have never come to the point of complete abandonment to His good will for you, there is never a better time than now.

Father,
> *Submitting to You seems risky, for You, rather than I, will be the one to direct my future from now on.*
> *Teach me to trust Your goodness and faithfulness.*
> *Take everything I am, and have, so that You and Your kingdom will be glorified in me.*

In Jesus' name, amen.

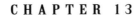

CHAPTER 13

Crucibles and Glory

"Father, the time has come. Glorify your Son,
that your Son may glorify you."
John 17:1

In the first six chapters we considered the difficult truth that our Father not only permits us to suffer but may actually lead us into situations in which He knows ahead of time that we will feel hurt. But it is not the doing of a vicious God who wishes to antagonize us. Rather it is the plan of a loving Father who responds to our own desires to see Himself fully reflected at the core of who we are. God designed human beings to display His character, so unless His character is restored within, we will never live as the glorious testimonies to the goodness and love of God that we were originally meant to reveal and enjoy. But we are desperately sinful people living in a desperately sinful world, and the process of restoration is rarely pleasant or easy.

In the past six chapters we have considered six graces, characteristics of God Himself, that are often matured within life's painful crucibles.

In this final chapter we return to a theme that we have touched on briefly throughout the book—the glory of God. I believe that the desire to honor and glorify the Father is the greatest longing that a human being can possess. It is the motivation that keeps us committed to reflecting Jesus in spite of the suffering that it may require.

However, I would now like to suggest that the glory and honor of God is so important that it is worth dying for—not just in a spiritual sense, but in reality. Indeed, the very giving up of a life within the providence of God may bring more honor and glory to Him than anything that might have been said or done while alive. So living for the glory of God always carries with it the call to offer ourselves utterly for Him, whatever it may cost.

Let's begin to see why.

The Great Controversy in a School Library

"The Columbine tragedy didn't start out as a front-page story about the battle between good and evil. But it has been moving there," wrote Nancy Gibbs in *Time*. "With each passing day of shock and grief you could almost hear the church bells tolling in the background, calling the country to a different debate, a careful conversation in which even presidents and anchormen behave as though they are in the presence of something bigger than they are, and maybe should lower their voices a little and speak with less authority.... But for those with an eye toward larger battles, the killers were not themselves evil; they were instruments of it, of the dark force we met in Narnia and try not to think about once we grow up, until the day we have no choice" (Nancy Gibbs, "Noon in the Garden of Good and Evil," *Time,* May 17, 1999).

The parents of Rachel Scott and Cassie Bernall, two of the Columbine victims, were absolutely certain that what happened at Columbine High School was the direct work of this evil. Both families believed that when Dylan Klebold and Eric Harris approached their daughters, their question was the same:

"Do you believe in God?"

Cassie is reported to have replied, "Yes." Rachel also said yes, to which the reply was "Then go be with Him."

Cassie's father, Brad Bernall, considers that Columbine was not just a random act of madness but a deliberate attack of Satan against Christians. In an interview Brad said, "I really believe that what happened at Columbine on that day was truly a spiritual battle. It was a pinnacle, and Satan was trying to make his stand, and God was going to reply, and He did." Brad went on to share the story of a boy who was eventually paralyzed from the waist down. The boy's mother told him that after her son was shot, a huge angel appeared in front of him, looked down and said, "Don't move. Just play dead." Seconds later one of the killers passed close by, paused, and walked on.

"I think I can address with some authority, more so, how it was really a spiritual battle," Brad continued, "because I was able to see the videotapes that Eric and Dylan made before they committed their crime. And in that, in that tape, it was very blatant they hated Christians, they hated God. That's mostly what they talked about. All the f-ing little Christians. And one thing that they said that really caught my ear was that they said they were going to shoot the Christians in the head" (from the DVD *They Sold Their Souls for Rock and Roll* [2003]).

Less than 12 months before the shooting, Rachel seemed to have an inkling of something strange on the horizon. She wrote in her diary, "This will be my last year, Lord. I have gotten what I can. Thank You."

In spite of the heartbreak and anguish, Cassie's mother, Misty, believed that God was still working out His good purposes. A few days after the murders she believed that He told her clearly, "Cassie was born for this" ("A Surge of Teen Spirit," *Time,* May 31, 1999). It was the message that she quickly began passing on to others.

Glory From Death?

Was Cassie born to die? Are some born to be witnesses to the world, after an ever-so-brief existence, in a martyr's death?

The challenge for us is that death always appears so final and non-negotiable. How then could death—which is the very curse of sin—have any redeeming value?

That problem confronts us in the story of Lazarus. Jesus loved him, and He loved his sisters, Mary and Martha. So after hearing that Lazarus was sick, Jesus stayed away until He knew that the brother was dead.

It was a strange response. How did Jesus think the sisters would react? He knew the tears that they would cry, the deep sorrow and loss that would claw at their hearts, the bitter questions that they would aim at Him and His Father. He recognized that they would be absolutely devastated.

When Jesus first heard about Lazarus' sickness He recognized a supreme purpose in it that would require a delay. "Jesus said, 'This sickness will not end in death. No, it is for God's glory so that God's Son may be glorified through it'" (John 11:4). Christ would demonstrate to all through the experience that He could bring a joy into their lives that could transform even the deepest, most profound disappointment of the human heart.

The tragedy of Lazarus' death ultimately revealed the glory of God. To those still wondering about the possibility of a future after death, the Lazarus story confirmed that there is someone in the universe who has the ability to reach down into our utter brokenness and bring back life, meaning, and purpose. But in the end it's still not just about finding wholeness for us. Rather, it's about the greatness of the God who can make it happen. It all points to Him.

In the meantime—in the waiting period between death and resurrection, as Jesus works for His Father's glory—He takes "risks." He "risked" alienating Mary and Martha in their crucible. Jesus may take the same "risk" with us as well.

God does not hide the potential cost for us as we pursue lives that glorify Him. For some people He calls for the total sacrifice of the martyr's death. Peter, perhaps like Rachel Scott, received a shadowy warning when Jesus said to him, "'I tell you the truth, when you were younger you dressed yourself and went where you wanted; but when you are old you will stretch out your hands, and someone else will dress you and lead you where you do not want to go.' Jesus said this to indicate the kind of death by which Peter would glorify God. Then he said to him, 'Follow me!'" (John 21:18, 19).

Can you imagine the impact of knowing this as the years rolled by? Jesus ensured that Peter would always see a literal crucifixion ahead.

What Is God's Glory?

Before we continue, perhaps we need to clarify what we mean by God's glory. It's one of those words that sounds important, but perhaps we're not too certain of its substance. The glory of God can have at least three meanings. It can stand for the physical brightness of His personal presence. We can use it as a synonym for His character. Or it can refer to the honor God receives from others. However, in this chapter we will consider (though unfortunately quite briefly) the glory of God in terms of the third meaning, God's honor.

A Model for Glorifying God

Jesus came to earth for the sole purpose of honoring the Father. In the following passages consider how His mission unfolded:

The arrival of Jesus to earth caused angels to sing to the Father's glory: "Glory to God in the highest, and on earth peace to men on whom his favor rests" (Luke 2:14).

The works of Jesus caused people to give the Father glory: "When he came near the place where the road goes down the Mount of Olives, the whole crowd of disciples began joyfully to praise God in loud voices for all the miracles they had seen: 'Blessed is the king who comes in the name of the Lord!' 'Peace in heaven and glory in the highest!'" (Luke 19:37, 38).

When Jesus' disciples bore fruit it glorified the Father: "This is to my Father's glory, that you bear much fruit, showing yourselves to be my disciples" (John 15:8).

Jesus' complete obedience to God's will brought the Father glory: "I have brought you glory on earth by completing the work you gave me to do" (John 17:4).

Jesus' death glorified the Father: "After Jesus said this, he looked toward heaven and prayed: 'Father, the time has come. Glorify your Son, that your Son may glorify you'" (verse 1).

When Jesus saved human beings, it glorified the Father: "In him we were also chosen, having been predestined according to the plan of him who works out everything in conformity with the purpose of his will, in order that we, who were the first to hope in Christ, might be for the praise of his glory. . . . Having believed, you were marked in him with a seal, the promised Holy Spirit, who is a deposit guaranteeing our inheritance until the redemption of those who are God's possession—to the praise of his glory" (Eph. 1:11-14).

When Jesus will be worshipped by all beings ever created, the Father will be glorified: "Therefore God exalted him to the highest place and gave him the name that is above every name, that at the name of Jesus every knee should bow, in heaven and on earth and under the earth, and every tongue confess that Jesus Christ is Lord, to the glory of God the Father" (Phil. 2:9-11).

At each step in the plan of salvation Jesus' life glorifies the Father. Jesus glorifies the Father because His downward path is at all times characterized by a self-sacrificing love that results in service, no matter the cost.

However, I would suggest that Jesus' willingness to offer Himself to serve others was not something He had to learn to do in order to deal with the sin problem. Rather service to others has been a God-glorifying principle that has shaped the Trinity itself and the government of heaven since eternity. And indeed, it will continue to guide the whole of heaven into eternity, because living to serve others no matter the cost is a principle that springs from God's very own nature. However, in the context of a world alienated from Him by sin, the application of this God-glorifying principle of selfless service would propel Jesus out of heaven and down into our dark earth to give up His own life for us.

Agents of Glory

While Jesus brought glory to His Father as He fulfilled His mission as the Father's Son, Jesus isn't the only one who has the privilege of bringing glory to the Father. Israel was also considered God's son. As God told Moses to say to Pharaoh: "Israel is my firstborn son, and I told you, 'Let my son go, so he may worship me'" (Ex. 4:22, 23). The purpose of Israel, as the son of God, was to bring glory to the Father. God revealed these intentions when He promised Abraham that "all peoples on earth will be blessed through you" (Gen. 12:3).

We too are part of this promise and intended blessing, for we are also sons, as Paul confirms: "You are all sons of God through faith in Christ Jesus" (Gal. 3:26). It seems that our purpose as His sons and daughters is also to bring glory to the Father. Paul writes again: "May the God who gives endurance and encouragement give you a spirit of unity among yourselves as you follow Christ Jesus, so that with one heart and mouth you may glorify the God and Father of our Lord Jesus Christ" (Rom. 15:5, 6). Indeed, "love for God, zeal for His glory, and love for fallen humanity brought Jesus to earth to suffer and to die. This was the controlling power of His life. This principle He bids us adopt" (Ellen G. White, *The Desire of Ages,* p. 330). Such zeal for the Father's glory may also compel us to offer ourselves utterly for others.

The Father is clearly the focus of our honoring, and Jesus, the Son of God, is our model in honoring Him as we imitate His willingness to sacrifice everything necessary to serve others. But let's return again to why honoring the Father is so important through the pages of the Bible.

Why Glorifying God Really Matters: The Story Behind the Story

In one sense the simple answer to why we glorify the Father is that the Father is unrivaled as the Creator of the universe. As David explains: "Great is the Lord and most worthy of praise; his greatness no one can fathom" (Ps. 145:3). But I think there is another, more specific reason for God to be glorified.

In chapter 4 we began to consider suffering in the context of the great battle between Satan and Jesus. We often see this conflict as simply a struggle between good and evil, but it is certainly more than that. In order to grasp the dynamics of this warfare, we need to understand what happened at the very beginning, long before the events of Genesis 1 unfolded.

The problem is that the Bible does not give many details about what took place in heaven as war broke out. We know that pride was at the root of Satan's rebellion, for he aspired to be as high as the uncreated Father (Isa. 14:12-15). As a result, a war broke out, and heaven had to cast out Satan and his angels (Rev. 12:7-9). We also know that the consequence of this expulsion is that we face an invisible and supernatural enemy (Eph. 6:11, 12) who will one day be totally destroyed (Rev. 20). But is there anything more that is helpful to know?

In the seventeenth century John Milton wrote about Lucifer's fall from heaven in his epic poem *Paradise Lost*. In a Harvard essay Gary Anderson highlights the main reasons for the fall of Satan as Milton describes it (Gary A. Anderson, "The Fall of Satan in the Thought of St. Ephrem and John Milton," *Hugoye: Journal of Syriac Studies* 3, no. 1 [January 2000]).

Anderson maintains that Milton saw a distinctive story emerging from texts such as Colossians 1:16; Psalm 2:6, 7; and Philippians 2:9, 10. Milton's plotline begins as Satan hears of a rumor that the Father and Son are planning to create humanity. As the highest created being in heaven, Satan feels hurt because the Godhead has not involved him in the discussions. Aware of this, the Father assembles all the angels and exalts Jesus above all to demonstrate that no one else could be compared to Him.

"If Satan found this objectionable and a cause for rebellion," Anderson observes, "then it is hardly idle speculation to say that he would have found the figures of Adam and Eve more objectionable. In some sense the elevation of Christ is a provoking moment that provides the necessary occasion for Satan to vent his hostility toward God's larger designs with His universe. The elevation of Christ smokes out the secret hatred of this formidable angel and foe" (*ibid.*).

In the 1870 publication *The Spirit of Prophecy,* volume 1, published 200 years after Milton's poem, Ellen White also describes the origins of this rebellion, and in a very similar way. She portrays how Satan was envious of Jesus' position and began to assume some of His authority himself. The Father then summoned all of heaven together to honor Jesus and to affirm His equality with Himself. All the angels bowed, including Satan.

Then she depicts what happened next. Satan left the presence of the Father jealous of Jesus. He began to suggest to the angels that the Father preferred Jesus and was ignoring him. As a result he claimed that God had trampled on his rights as the leader of the angels and that the angels would inevitably suffer under the leadership of Jesus. He, Satan, was going to oppose such a possibility. And so "they rebelled against the authority of the Son.

"Angels that were loyal and true sought to reconcile this mighty, rebellious angel to the will of his Creator. . . . They clearly set forth that Jesus was the Son of God, existing with Him before the angels were created; and that He had ever stood at the right hand of God, and His mild, loving authority had not heretofore been questioned; and that He had given no commands but what it was joy for the heavenly host to execute. . . .

"Satan refused to listen. And then he turned from the loyal and true angels, denouncing them as slaves. . . . Satan unblushingly made known his dissatisfaction that Christ should be preferred before him. He stood up proudly and urged that he should be equal with God, and should be taken into conference with the Father and understand His purposes. God informed Satan that to his Son alone He would reveal His secret purposes, and He required all the family in heaven, even Satan, to yield him implicit, unquestioned obedience; but that he [Satan] had proved himself unworthy a place in heaven. Then Satan exultingly pointed to his sympathizers, comprising nearly one half of all the angels, and exclaimed, These are with me! Will you expel these also, and make such a void in heaven? He then declared that he was prepared to resist the authority of Christ, and to defend his place in heaven by force of might, strength against strength" (*The Spirit of Prophecy* [Battle Creek, Mich.: Seventh-day Adventist Pub. Assn., 1870], vol. 1, pp. 18-24).

Glorifying God Today

This background focuses our attention on some of the finer issues in the great controversy story. Most important, it helps us to understand the relationship between our crucibles and God's glory as we walk the often rocky path toward the Shepherd's house. Here we encounter two issues that emerge as highly significant for those desiring to live lives committed to glorifying the Father.

First, we glorify the Father through discipleship to His Son. The rebellion that emerged in heaven began with the personal animosity of Satan toward Jesus. Jesus Himself was the focus of Satan's irritation and rebellion. Because the Father and Son made humanity in Their image, we become the secondary object of Satan's anger. So if Satan can tempt us away from God, he can hurt the Father and the Son. By choosing to remain a disciple of Jesus, we honor the Father. The more we imitate the Son, the more we glorify the Father. It's not a coincidence, therefore, that our primary discipleship is to Jesus. Jesus has always been the focus of Satan's jealousy and the one that he desires to replace. As we increasingly reflect the character of Jesus, we are again making a choice, not simply for a good way to live, but for the true Lord of our lives.

Second, we glorify the Father through obedience to His government. As a consequence of Satan's personal animosity to Jesus, the devil tries to discredit the authority of the Father and the law on which His government is based. We therefore glorify the Father by the way we live. The Bible reveals to us the laws, principles, and values of the kingdom of heaven. As we incorporate them into real life, we are not simply following instructions in order to find personal fulfillment. We obey because we are making a conscious choice to honor the government of the Father, and to reject the "freedoms" that Satan offers by bringing the kingdom of God to earth.

Here is where things become challenging. As culture becomes increasingly hostile to the true character of God and tries more and more to oppose His kingdom, those who remain committed to a God-glorifying life may find that remaining in loyal service to the Father will require the sacrifice of their lives.

Glorifying God in the Future

Rachel Scott's father, Darrell, told a group in Little Rock, Arkansas, "'God is using this tragedy to wake up not only America but also the world.' . . . 'God is using Rachel as a vehicle'" (S. C. Gwynne, "An Act of God?" *Time,* Dec. 20, 1999). Based on the news reports, the murders of the Columbine Christians really seemed to have stirred a revival among thousands of evangelical youth. And in the end, God was being glorified.

In describing the progress of history, John writes about martyrs past and martyrs future: "When he opened the fifth seal, I saw under the altar the souls of those who had been slain because of the word of God and the testimony they had maintained. They called out in a loud voice, 'How long, Sovereign Lord, holy and true, until you judge the inhabitants of the earth and avenge our blood?' Then each of them was given a white robe, and they were told to wait a little longer, until the number of their fellow servants and brothers who were to be killed as they had been was completed" (Rev. 6:9-11).

When we read such passages we think about individuals dying at a fiery stake hundred of years ago, not teenage girls with laptops looking down the barrel of a sawed-off shotgun. But Revelation certainly believes that more is to come.

Facing the possibility of the stake, the great reformer John Huss wrote to his friends in Prague, "Why, then, should we not suffer also, particularly when suffering is for us a purification? Therefore, beloved, if my death ought to contribute to His glory, pray that it may come quickly, and that He may enable me to support all my calamities with constancy" (in Ellen G. White, *The Great Controversy,* p. 105).

Martyrdom did come to Huss, but he wasn't fearful. "When the flames kindled about him, he began to sing, 'Jesus, Thou Son of David, have mercy on me,' and so continued till his voice was silenced forever.

"Even his enemies were struck with his heroic bearing. A zealous papist, describing the martyrdom of Huss, and of Jerome, who died soon after, said: 'Both bore themselves with constant mind when their last hour approached. They prepared for the fire as if they were going to a marriage feast. They uttered no cry of pain. When the flames rose, they began to sing hymns; and scarce could the vehemency of the fire stop their singing'" (*ibid.*, pp. 109, 110).

Can you imagine a greater way for the Father and Son to be glorified than that? Despite the greatest crucibles that Satan can concoct, the Father still provides His people with a song that bears witness to His power and goodness for centuries.

Searching for a Life That Glorifies

Rachel Scott, Cassie Bernall, John Huss, and the thousands of martyrs throughout history knew that honoring the Father was worth more than life itself. I think God has given all of us an instinct towards glorifying Him, though our search for it may not always be clearly understood, nor the Power that leads us. We search to understand the greater but mysterious heavenly power at work around us, but we often fail to grasp it. In a highly personal piece entitled "A Note for Rachel Scott" journalist Roger Rosenblatt seems to reflect such a quest.

Rosenblatt refers to one of the interviews that Rachel's father gave after her murder. In the interview, Darrell Scott stated that the many legal and governmental questions asked after Columbine did not touch "the deep issues of the heart." In his article Rosenblatt comments that "the deep issue I want to touch upon has to do with me and my colleagues—journalists who, for all our recurrent, usually unattractive displays of know-it-all confidence, occasionally come upon a story such as yours [Rachel's] and recognize our helplessness before it.... So, Rachel, when I write, 'This is what I want to tell you,' please read, 'This is what

I want to ask': Where do we, who ply our trade in this magazine and elsewhere, find the knowledge of the unknowable? How do we learn to trust the unknowable as news—those deep issues of the heart? The problem belongs both to us and to those we hope to serve. Journalists are pretty good at unearthing the undeep issues. Give us a presidential scandal, even a war, and we can do a fair job of explaining the explicable. But give us the killings at Columbine, and in an effort to cover the possibilities we will miss what people are thinking in their secret chambers—thinking, feeling—about their own loves and hatreds, about the necessity of attentiveness to others, about their own children: about *you, Rachel*" (Roger Rosenblatt, "A Note for Rachel Scott," *Time,* May 10, 1999).

I don't think Rosenblatt is the only one searching for answers concerning the "deep things." Tragedies often make us speechless as we pause a moment to catch our breath. But in this book I hope I have been able to convey to you the good news that Christians do have a response to even the harshest crucibles that can, in time, bring peace, hope, and spiritual maturity. And this can happen even when life appears unknowable.

Perhaps no one has articulated the redemption of hope from despair better than Paul. As he writes to the Corinthians, he touches on many of the things we have already examined: the overwhelming crucibles that greet us on the path, yet the resilience that is possible because the deep things of God are within us. In spite of our brokenness, God's Spirit is always aiming to keep our eyes fixed on Jesus, so that His character—His gold—may find a place in us, and thus prove a compelling testimony to an ever-loving Father, a compassionate Savior, and a way of living marked by the imprint and presence of heaven.

"But we have this treasure in jars of clay to show that this all-surpassing power is from God and not from us. We are hard pressed on every side, but not crushed; perplexed, but not in despair; persecuted, but not abandoned; struck down, but not destroyed. We always carry around in our body the death of Jesus, so that the life of Jesus may also be revealed in our body. For we who are alive are always being given over to death for Jesus' sake, so that his life may be revealed in our body. … With that same spirit of faith we also believe and therefore speak, because we know that the one who raised the Lord Jesus from the dead will also raise us with Jesus and present us with you in his presence. All this is for your benefit, so that the grace that is reaching more and more people may cause thanksgiving to overflow to the glory of God. Therefore we do not lose heart. Though outwardly we are wasting away, yet inwardly we are being renewed day by day. For our light and momentary troubles are achieving for us an eternal glory that far out-weighs them all. So we fix our eyes not on what is seen, but on what is unseen. For what is seen is temporary, but what is unseen is eternal" (2 Cor. 4:7-18).

Father,
    Grant me a mind that is single for Your glory;
    A heart that longs to honor You, no matter what life throws across my path;
    Eyes that continually search for the risen Christ,
    That I may reflect Him more and more.
In His name, amen.